D0355678

Secret
NEW YORK

NEW YORK

Exploring the City's
Hidden Neighborhoods

by Michelle Haimoff
photography by Rachel Feierman

Interlink Books

An imprint of Interlink Publishing Group, Inc.
Northampton, Massachusetts

First published in 2008 by

INTERLINK TRAVEL
An imprint of Interlink Publishing Group, Inc.
46 Crosby Street, Northampton, Massachusetts 01060
www.interlinkbooks.com

Copyright © Interlink Travel, 2008
Text copyright © Michelle Haimoff, 2008
Photography copyright © Rachel Feierman, 2008
Maps by Jacob Shemkovitz

Library of Congress Cataloging-in-Publication Data
Haimoff, Michelle.
Secret New York / by Michelle Haimoff. — 1st American ed.
p. cm.
Includes bibliographical references.
ISBN-13: 978-1-56656-672-8 (pbk. : alk. paper)
ISBN-10: 1-56656-672-X (pbk. : alk. paper)
1. New York (N.Y.)—Tours. 2. New York Region—Tours. 3. Historic
buildings—New York (State)—New York—Guidebooks. 4. Historic
sites—New York (State)—New York—Guidebooks. 5. Walking—New
York (State)—New York—Guidebooks. 6. New York (N.Y.)—Buildings,
structures, etc.—Guidebooks. I. Title.
F128.18.H325 2007
917.47'10444—dc22

2006031038

Back cover author photo by Pauline Shapiro

Printed and bound in China

To request our complete 40-page full-color catalog,
please call us toll free at 1-800-238-LINK, visit our website at
www.interlinkbooks.com or write to Interlink Publishing
46 Crosby Street, Northampton, MA 01060
e-mail: info@interlinkbooks.com

Contents

Acknowledgments

I'd like to acknowledge the help of the following organizations and individuals with the research in this book:

    The Central Park Conservancy
    The Corcoran Group
    The Eldridge Street Project
    IDG Jewelers
    The Municipal Arts Society
    Rachel Feierman Photography

I'd also like to thank Hilary Plum for her meticulous editing job, as well as certified New Yorkers Orly Cooper, Rachel Feierman, Abigail Ford, Carley Graham, Emily Heyward, Lauren Schnipper, Pauline Shapiro, and Emily Wallach, whose input and friendship contribute to every endeavor. Thanks also to my friends and family for their support.

Key to Maps

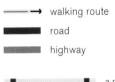

→ walking route

road

highway

building of interest

park / garden of interest

other area of interest

a note on scale:

A standard New York City block is exactly 1/20 of a mile, or 264 feet, on its narrow side. So, for example, a five block span is equal to a quarter mile.

List of Maps

Introduction

New York is called "the city that never sleeps" because at any given hour of the night windows glow with signs of life. As the most densely populated area of the country, approximately 1 in 37 American residents live in New York City, which means that when you are here you are never alone. You're surrounded by tossers and turners, partiers and worriers, artists, tycoons, and visionaries. The taxis and subways never stop running. The street noise never dies down. Restaurants serve duck confit in the middle of the night. Something or someone is always being built up or torn down and it is virtually impossible to keep up with the latest that the city has to offer.

It seems there can't be any mystery left in New York because there isn't even enough of the city to go around. The space is so highly coveted that every square foot is accounted for. New York has some of the most expensive real estate in the world simply because of the insatiable demand for it. This part of the country might as well have its own currency because anyone who wants to live here must be willing to sacrifice space, privacy, and logic, not to mention cash, for a share of the city that everyone claims but no one owns.

Manhattan is not only a small island but also a small world. Locals keep in touch with friends simply by walking around the street on a nice day. It is amazing how long New Yorkers can go without seeing anyone they know, but it is even more amazing how often they run into everyone they've ever met. The community is one you have to be a part of to understand, simultaneously aloof and profoundly connected, like a family that has been together too long for formality. Strangers will ask your opinion, or compliment your shoes, or try to fix you up with their son, all while waiting for a walk sign. As with any family, if you stick around long enough, you'll find that you're a part of it whether you like it or not.

Oddly, despite their attachment to the city and to each other, New Yorkers tend to be unaware of the history, beauty, and intrigue that exist on every corner. Residents are too preoccupied to look around, while tourists are generally too focused on the key attractions to delve deeper into the world that exists beneath the urban landscape: the hidden gardens and back alleys, secret art installations and unmarked speakeasies, havens of solitude and entire islands where locals dare not tread. Even the obvious sights have lesser-known histories that are rarely revealed, and behind the iconic buildings and monuments are the underground stories and struggles that have made this city all things to all people.

More than any other city in the world, New York lends itself to walking tours because of its pedestrian culture. Because the entire length of Manhattan is only 13.4 miles, New York is the kind of place you can wander for hours and never run out of things to see. Each neighborhood has the feel of a small town with its own particular character and charm. I am certain that whatever tour you go on, however long you've been living in the city, you will see and learn something you never knew existed.

Enjoy the journey.

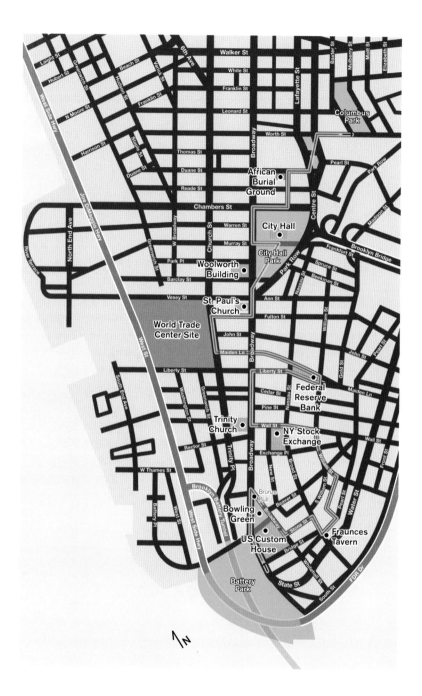

Lower Manhattan

ower Manhattan is where it all begins. The archaeological ruins of America's former capital are here, as well as the core of the city's governmental and financial mechanisms. The neighborhood has changed considerably over the years, but streets are still identified by name rather than number. Beaver Street was named for its beaver exchange, Broad Street once held a canal, Stone Street employed the city's first paving stones, Church Street was named for St. Paul's Chapel, Baxter Street referred to a prominent butcher, and Pearl Street was named for iridescent oyster shells strewn across the original shoreline.

The city's history evolves with its geography, and since New York was one of the first colonies to be settled, the southernmost tip of Manhattan Island is not only rich in local history, but also in early American history. It was here that English explorer Henry Hudson landed in 1609 while seeking out the Northwest Passage; it was here that generations of the city's immigrants commenced their journey as Americans; and it was here that the United States became a great shipping power, and ultimately a major player in the world economy.

The Lower Manhattan Walk

Start:	Battery Park entrance
Finish:	Columbus Park
Length:	2 miles
Time:	1.5 hours

Refreshments: Battery Gardens for upscale dining, river views, and casual refreshments; Stone Street has a number of cute outdoor restaurants, including American eatery AJ Kelly; Zigolinis Famiglia serves well-priced make-your-own pastas and salads; Les Halles Downtown offers hearty French food and sandwiches.

Sights: Battery Park, Castle Clinton, US Customs House, Bowling Green, Fraunces Tavern, Stone Street, Delmonico's, the Bank of New York, Federal Hall, the "House of Morgan," New York Stock Exchange, Trinity Church, Equitable Building, Chamber of Commerce, Liberty Tower, Federal Reserve Bank of New York, Maiden Lane, World Trade Center site, St. Paul's Chapel, City Hall and Park, Woolworth Building, A.T. Stewart Department Store, Municipal Building, Tweed Courthouse, African Burial Ground, Five Points.

Note: Tours of the Federal Reserve Bank must be booked at least one week in advance.

B attery Park is located at the narrowest point of Manhattan Island. The 23-acre park was named after the battery of guns the Dutch used to defend their colony in the seventeenth century. As you walk through the park you'll come to "the Sphere," which stood in the plaza of the World Trade Center as a symbol of world peace. The sculpture was moved here as a memorial to the destruction of the Twin Towers. Castle Clinton, at the far end of the park, was built in 1811 to protect New York's harbor during the War of 1812. By 1824, the castle was converted into a public garden and aquarium.

As you exit Battery Park, walk toward the imposing Smithsonian National Museum of the American Indian and former **US Customs House**. Directly across the brick-paved road from the museum's entrance is Bowling Green. Bowling Green was originally a Native American tribal gathering place and the likely site of Manhattan's purchase. The Dutch literally used the green as a bowling spot, and in 1733 the British used it as their first public park in the American colonies. A statue of King George III stood here until July 9, 1776, when independence was declared in New York and an angry mob tore it down, but the original fence surrounding the green has been

here since 1771. Directly behind Bowling Green is the spirited bronze bull that has come to characterize the financial district. The 7,000-pound bull was left here anonymously in 1989 after Italian artist Arturo DeModica failed to sell it as a work of art. Police arrested and impounded the bull, but the public petitioned to bring him back. The bull was granted this space temporarily but no attempts have been made to move him since. Perhaps that is because in the 1990s, the bull, which symbolizes a market charging upward, is seen to have brought on one of the longest bull runs in American history.

Walk down Broadway and make a left onto Stone Street. The austere building at 85 Broad in front of you is the Goldman Sachs building, one of the many financial institutions in the area. Turn right and make a left at Bridge Street. The Revolutionary War–era **Fraunces Tavern** is on your right. Walk down Pearl Street and glance into the eighteenth-century wells enclosed in bronze railings, with tablets describing their historical significance. Turn left on Coenties Alley and turn right to get back onto Stone Street, which faces the back of 85 Broad. This landmark historic district turns into a lively outdoor happy hour scene in the warmer months.

Turn left at William Street and glance at Delmonico's on Beaver Street to your left, the country's first café and pastry shop. The 1836 building, supported by pillars from the Roman ruins of Pompeii, is actually the third incarnation since Giovanni and Pietro Delmonico started their business in 1827. A former men's-only hotel and restaurant, the establishment also served as a meeting spot for the country's first all-women's club, "Sorosis," in 1868.

Stop at Wall Street and take in the Bank of New York directly across from you. The Bank of New York was Secretary of Treasury Alexander Hamilton's bank and the exclusive bank of New York State. Hamilton's adversary, Aaron Burr, wanted to open a bank of his own but the state prohibited it, so he started a water company instead. The stated purpose of Burr's corporation was to bring fresh water into New York City, the demand for which was especially high as a result of the recent yellow fever epidemic. However, the charter's fine print also enabled Burr to lend out the company's profits, effectively making his company a bank as well. Burr's Manhattan Water Company eventually merged with Chase to become the Chase-Manhattan Bank. Ironically, Chase-Manhattan once resided at the Trump Building on Wall Street adjacent to Hamilton's Bank of New York.

Walk down Wall Street, the "wall" of which was nothing more than a twelve-foot-high log barricade built by slaves in 1653. Spanning Manhattan Island river to river, pieces of it were often stolen for firewood. The physical wall was demolished in 1699, but the street name remains. George Washington was inaugurated in the former Federal Hall building in 1789 on the very spot where his likeness stands. Congress also met here for the first time and it was here that they ratified the Bill of Rights. The building is now a museum, with such American relics as George Washington's inaugural bible. Look to your left to see the "House of Morgan," the intentionally nondescript building on the eastern corner with the very large windows. The building is unmarked because billionaire financier J.P. Morgan didn't want to do business with those who didn't know who he was. He also used only four stories of the very expensive real estate to show that he was wealthy enough to forgo the rent that his property could have accrued if the building were taller. In 1920, an Italian anarchist in a horse-drawn carriage bombed the building, killing 33 civilians. This was the worst act of terrorism in the country until the Oklahoma City bombing of 1995. If you look closely, you'll see that the walls are still scarred with pockmarks from the explosion.

The building on the western corner is the New York Stock Exchange. The New York Stock Exchange building was completed in 1903, but the exchange itself was founded in 1792, when a group of 24 brokers met under a sycamore tree at Broad and Wall Streets to trade stocks and securities. The sculpture on top of the building by famous artist John Quincy Adams Ward is entitled "Integrity Protecting the Works of

Man," "Integrity" being the figure in the center. The sculpture was once restored in secret so that no one would notice that integrity had deteriorated.

Keep walking down Wall Street to **Trinity Church**. Make a right at the church and walk up Broadway. Notice the bronze strips embedded in the ground. Broadway was a ticker-tape parade route and these plaques commemorate those for whom the parades were thrown. Across Broadway between Pine and Cedar Street is the Equitable Building, so named because its eight-story height surpassed the five-story height limit of the other buildings in its day. In 1872, the building was one of the first to use a working elevator. Turn right at Liberty Street and walk down to the Chamber of Commerce building on Liberty Place. Since the American Revolution, portraits of 200 American leaders have been amassed here and are on display in the Great Hall. The Liberty Tower across the street was President Franklin Delano Roosevelt's workplace in the 1920s before his political career began. Follow Liberty Street past the Federal Reserve Bank of New York, with bars on its arched windows. Woodrow Wilson established this "bank for banks" as part of a 1913 act to create a centralized banking system. The structure before you holds $60 billion in solid gold, stored five stories under the ground.

At the black abstract sculpture on William Street, make a sharp left onto Maiden Lane, named for the Dutch maidens that washed and laundered clothing here in colonial times. The cobblestone road was also a spot for romantic walks after dark. There is a historic plaque on 57 Maiden Lane where third president Thomas Jefferson lived in 1790. It was here that Jefferson and Secretary of Treasury Alexander Hamilton agreed to make Washington, DC the nation's capital. Follow this street all the way down to Liberty Plaza and the **World Trade Center** site. As the construction progresses, a history of the area and a timeline of September 11, 2001 are on display.

Looking uptown, the tall building to your right is the Woolworth Building. At the corner of Church and Fulton, make a right and then turn left onto Broadway, where you'll see **St. Paul's Chapel**. This is the highest elevation point downtown.

Continue walking up Broadway and cross over to City Hall Park on Barclay Street. Walk straight through the park, past the fountains, until you can see City Hall. In the late 1700s, City Hall Park was the northernmost end of Manhattan and nothing more than a common area with a prison. But it is also the spot where George Washington read the Declaration of Independence on July 9, 1776, to an audience of Continental troops and American citizens. City Hall itself was built in 1812 and has provided offices for every elected New York mayor and City Council member. A statue of Revolutionary War hero Nathan Hale in shackles stands to your right. Hanged by the British in September 1776, the twenty-year-old spy famously proclaimed, "I regret that I have only one life to give for my country."

Exit the park to the west of the fountain and cross over to the **Woolworth Building**. The lobby alone is one of the most spectacular of any office building in the city and security can be tight, but try to at least get a peek at the building's interior. Follow Broadway to Chambers Street, where you'll see a seven-story building with windows that get progressively smaller at each level. This was originally the Sun Building, as you can tell by "the Sun" clock hanging off the corner. It was also home to the first department store, the **A.T. Stewart Store**, and the first commercial building in New York with a marble façade.

Turn right at Chambers. The building directly in front of you is the Municipal Building and the courthouse to your right is the Tweed Courthouse. The Municipal Building is where couples get married when they go to "City Hall." The ornamentation at the four corners represents the outer boroughs:

Brooklyn, the Bronx, Queens, and Staten Island. The 24-karat gold sculpture at the top entitled *Civic Fame* symbolizes Manhattan, and is the largest statue in the city. The Tweed Courthouse, formally known as the New York County Courthouse, was a $250,000 project that ended up costing the city millions: in the 1860s, the corrupt politician William Marcy Tweed stole hundreds of millions of dollars from the city for supposed municipal projects and then distributed the money among his friends. Emigrant Industrial Savings Bank on the north side of the street was one of the strongest banks in the city during the Great Depression because, as a depository for hard-up immigrants, the bank took very small deposits that no other bank would take.

Walk north on Elk Street, continuing all the way to Duane, and make another left. The fenced-in grassy square on the corner is an African Burial Ground,

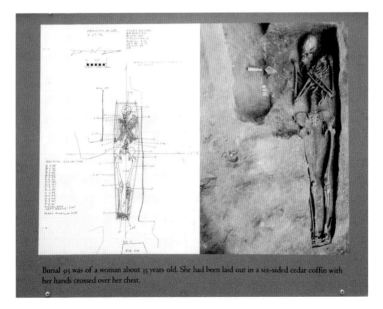

Burial 315 was of a woman about 35 years old. She had been laid out in a six-sided cedar coffin with her hands crossed over her chest.

which was unearthed during construction of the Federal Office Building at 290 Broadway in 1991. 419 remains facing Africa and adorned with African artifacts were discovered, and archeologists estimate that 20,000 slaves and free blacks were buried here between 1600s and 1795. Forty percent of those buried here were children under the age of twelve, most of whom were less than one year old. Walk east on Duane Street toward Federal Plaza, where you'll see the appellate courthouse and the Supreme Court to the left, the setting for many scenes from the popular crime show *Law & Order*. Walk through Foley Square, through the bronze medallions depicting the area's history, and past the fountain, until you come to Columbus Park at the intersection of Worth and Baxter. This was once the location of the notorious **Five Points** slum, but today Columbus Park is a lively community haven with a playground.

US Customs House

The Alexander Hamilton US Customs House is a three-block building built in 1907, designed to evoke an aura of wealth and authority. Before the 1916 income tax, customs duties formed the majority of the country's revenue source, and the port of New York was the country's principal trading center, so it was only fitting that the customs house be magnificent. Cass Gilbert, also the architect of the Woolworth Building, designed this Beaux Arts building, and Daniel Chester French sculpted the statuary; he later crafted the Lincoln Memorial in Washington, DC. Each of the 44 columns is topped with the head of Mercury, Roman god of speed and commerce, and the four seated figures represent "Four Continents," from left to right: Asia, America, Europe, and Africa. Note the American figure leaping out of her throne, symbolizing the United States breaking through in the twentieth century. If you get a chance to glance around inside, you'll see that the artwork on the interior is as impressive as the statuary on the exterior. The building is located on the site of Fort Amsterdam, which the Dutch built on the tip of the island to protect their colony, and where Dutch Governor Peter Stuyvesant eventually surrendered to the British. Today the building houses the Smithsonian National Museum of the American Indian and has the largest collection of Native American artifacts in the world.

FRAUNCES TAVERN

This tavern is a 1906 recreation of a 1762 Revolution era tavern run by Samuel Fraunces. A member of the anti-British Sons of Liberty, Fraunces ran this inn throughout the Revolutionary War into the city's first years as America's capital, and later lent his tavern to the provincial Congress of New York. The building housed the Departments of War, Treasury, and Foreign Affairs, but the Tavern is perhaps best known for General George Washington's emotional farewell address on the night of December 4, 1783, before returning to Virginia after his military victory. Today Fraunces Tavern houses a museum with colonial-era artifacts, weapons, and documents, but its role as a symbol of revolution has made it a target of violence: in 1974, radical Puerto Rican separatists bombed the tavern, killing four people.

TRINITY CHURCH

The first Trinity Church was destroyed in a fire and the second by a blizzard; this is the third. Built in 1846, this church was the tallest building in New York for 50 years. It was also considered one of the most vulgar, but the once seemingly drab brownstone is now thought to add to the architectural splendor of the structure. Trinity is the wealthiest church in the world, in no small part because of its initial land grant by Queen Anne of England, who bestowed the church all land from this site west to the Hudson River, north to Christopher Street, and south to Wall Street. Throughout the years, the church has benefited from selling and renting portions of this extensive land to other churches.

The first chief justice of the Supreme Court, John Jay, is buried in the cemetery, along with New York University founder Albert Gallatin and the first secretary of the treasury, Alexander Hamilton. Hamilton's death set a precedent for the church whereby anyone killed in a duel could not be buried in its cemetery. This is because Vice President Aaron Burr shot and killed the secretary of the treasury in a duel in 1804 in New Jersey (the duel could not take

place in New York, since Hamilton had pushed for a law banning dueling here when his own son had died this way). The white obelisk on the south side of the cemetery marks Hamilton's grave, and the church museum inside contains recreations of the pistols Alexander Hamilton and Aaron Burr used to settle their score.

WORLD TRADE CENTER SITE

Japanese-American architect Minoru Yamasaki built the modern-style office towers in 1977, each of which was over 100 feet higher than the mast of the Empire State Building. This made the World Trade Center buildings the tallest and largest in the world until 1974, when Chicago's Sears Tower surpassed them. Because the land on which the towers were built was landfill, the skyscrapers had to extend 70 feet underground in order to rest on bedrock. The underground area was used as a shopping mall, parking area, and underground rail. The majority of the building served as office space, mostly for financial firms, but One World Trade Center featured an upscale restaurant called Windows on the World. From the 1,300-foot-high observation deck of Two

World Trade Center, it was possible to see 45 miles in every direction. The complex was so vast it even had its own zip code. After terrorists flew two commercial airplanes into the World Trade Center on September 11, 2001, the towers collapsed, killing 2,749 people. Yet the structural integrity of the steel and concrete buildings, which allowed them to stand for over an hour after they had been hit, saved tens of thousands of lives. The loss of the World Trade Center drastically altered the New York skyline, and caused New Yorkers to reevaluate not only their sense of security, but also the oft-overlooked contemporary architecture that shapes the city's identity.

St. Paul's Chapel

Built in 1766, the church is New York's oldest public building in continual use. George Washington prayed here on the day of his inauguration in 1789, and above his private pew hangs an oil painting of the Great Seal of the United States. The glass windows are frosted because stained glass hadn't yet been invented, and the fourteen Waterford chandeliers, which hang in the nave and galleries, are the originals imported from Ireland in 1802. After the attack on the World Trade Center, the church served as a relief spot for recovery workers. Volunteers worked twelve-hour shifts for eight months, attending to the needs of the police, construction workers, and firefighters who lived out of this church while battling the debris.

Woolworth Building

Prominent architect Cass Gilbert completed Frank Woolworth's "Cathedral of Commerce" in 1913. At 792 feet, it was the world's tallest building until 1930 and one of its most ornately designed. Hoping that the building would inspire confidence and establish the permanence of his brand, Woolworth openly paid $15.5 million in cash for its construction. The carvings inside include Gilbert with a model building and F.W.

Woolworth counting his nickels. At the time of construction, heat-producing incandescent light bulbs were the only ones in use, and the architectural touch of a light court in the middle of the building allowed workers to avoid sweltering under these bulbs. On the night of its completion, President Woodrow Wilson turned on all 80,000 internal and external light bulbs from a switch in the White House.

A.T. Stewart Store

Alexander Stewart opened the city's first department store in 1846, introducing the type of shopping where customers could walk in freely and browse the items on display instead of waiting for the help of a clerk. The store also marked the beginning of ready-made clothing, at the time manufactured by immigrants in the building's top two floors, and the first time clothing was featured in windows to attract the attention of passersby. By the 1860s, Stewart's revolutionary shopping method was replicated by many other retail stores and had made him one of the wealthiest men in the city.

Five Points

Columbus Park was the epicenter of the Five Points slum, the worst slum in Western history. The slum was named Five Points for the five streets that converged to form it: Mulberry, Anthony (now Worth), Cross, Orange (now Baxter), and Little Water. The land started out as a large pond that served as a water source for its Native American inhabitants. The city drained the pond in the 1820s in order to convert the space into a suburban development called "Paradise Square." When houses started to sink, the rich inhabitants took off and the neighborhood declined into a dilapidated slum. Garbage, manure, and urine accumulated, only ever attended to by pigs. Telephone wires blocked out the sun, and immigrants lived in filthy, ankle-deep water with air so badly contaminated by the tuberculosis epidemic that residents had to keep their windows closed on even the hottest summer days. By 1832, 100 people died of typhoid-infected water every day in this neighborhood alone. Local thugs passed around menus of injury, which itemized violence by price, ranging from $5 for a sliced-off ear to $100 for murder. It is not surprising that New York City police officers never came here in groups of less than ten. Prostitution and alcoholism flourished around the

"Den of Thieves" brewery at the center of the Five Points, and affluent members of society went on tours entitled "How the Other Half Lives." By the 1890s, the area was converted to a park, and it is now a popular grassy retreat of the Chinatown community.

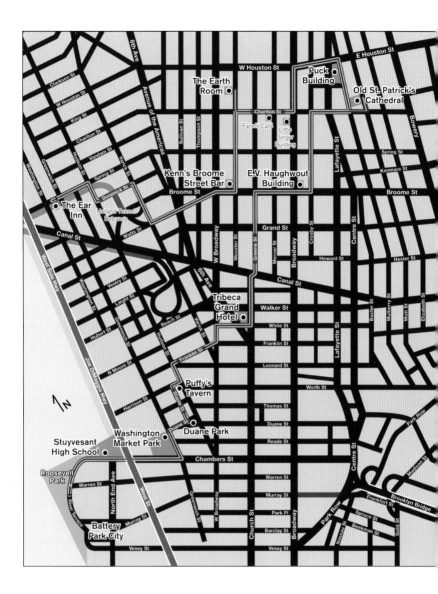

SoHo and Tribeca

The two most famous acronyms in Manhattan are SoHo, which is short for "south of Houston" and Tribeca, which stands for the "Triangle Below Canal." The neighborhoods are most famous for their run as artists' quarters starting in the 1950s, when abstract expressionists such as Mark Rothko, Franz Kline, and Jackson Pollock used the bright and airy commercial spaces for their work with large canvases. Prior to its artistic resurgence, SoHo and Tribeca served as industrial centers for dry goods and textiles, and you'll notice faded advertisements for writing, printing, and publishing materials painted on the buildings.

The waterfront near Tribeca was once New York's main food distribution center, with a large wholesale market and food warehouses. By the 1990s, rents had become increasingly expensive, and artists started to move out of this enclave and into Chelsea, Brooklyn, and other parts of the city. At the same time, upscale boutiques, cafés, and restaurants started moving in. The wide sidewalks and relatively low buildings make this neighborhood one of the nicer areas to stroll through, while the enormous windows and high ceilings make it one of the more expensive parts of the city to live in.

The SoHo and Tribeca Walk

Start:	Spring Street between Washington and Greenwich
Finish:	Battery Park City
Length:	2 miles
Time:	2 hours

Refreshments: The Ear Inn for pub food, Lupe's for low priced Mexican, Tennessee Mountain for BBQ, Jerry's for family-friendly American, or Balthazar for French bistro food and celebrity sightings.

Sights: The Ear Inn, Holland Tunnel, Kenn's Broome Street Bar, the New York Earth Room, Cast Iron District, Fanelli Café, Little Singer Building, Cable Building, Old St. Patrick Cathedral, E.V. Haughwout Building, the Gunther Building, the "Queen of Greene Street," AT&T Long Lines Building, Tribeca Grand Hotel, Western Union Building, Washington Market Park, Stuyvesant High School, Battery Park City.

The Ear Inn on Spring Street between Washington and Greenwich is one of the most authentic relics of old New York. If you're stopping here for a bite, try the chicken pot pie; it's one of their better dishes. As you exit the tavern, walk east on Spring Street until you get to Hudson. At Hudson, turn right. Cody's Bar & Grill, on the corner of Hudson and Dominick, sits in a building that dates back to the 1880s. In the 1970s, actor/comedian John Belushi rented the space as his own private club. Turn left on Dominick Street and right onto Varick. You'll pass the Holland Tunnel entrance on your right, which connects New York and New Jersey. The tunnel, which was completed after seven years of construction in 1927, was named for its chief engineer, Clifford M. Holland.

Turn left on Watts, where you'll see an enormous building on the southeast corner of Varick Street. A famous children's stomach remedy known as Castoria was manufactured here in the 1870s. Continue east on Watts, crossing Sixth Avenue, where down the block to your right you'll see the 1930s Moondance Diner. This former railroad dining car serves food around the clock on Thursday, Friday, and Saturday nights. Stay on Watts, past Thompson Street, until you get to Broome. Kenn's Broome Street Bar on the corner operates out of an original 1825 Federal-style house. Back when this was an artists' neighborhood, painters ranging from Willem de Kooning to Keith Haring hung out here. Follow Broome to Wooster Street and turn left. You'll notice a plethora of clothing boutiques, design stores, and even the occasional art gallery. The Christopher Fisher store on your right was one of the first artist's studios in SoHo, belonging to fluxus artist and political activist George Maciuna in the 1960s. Continuing past Spring and Prince streets, you'll see a nondescript gray building on your immediate left, across the street from the Stüssy store. #141 Wooster Street holds the New York Earth Room, an interior earth sculpture that has been on view to the public since 1980. The exhibit's hours are erratic, but entrance is free; simply buzz #2B to check it out.

Back on Prince, walk east toward Broadway and take note of an old advertisement for a lithographic company above 120 Prince. This neighborhood is the largest **Cast Iron District** in the world. The Mimi Ferzt Gallery building is one of many examples you'll see of cast iron architecture. Following Prince Street, you'll find some of the most alluring street vendors in the city. As with any outdoor market, all prices are negotiable, so try to resist the seller's first offer. Fanelli Café on the corner of Mercer is named for its former owner, Michael Fanelli, a one-time boxer who held onto the bar for 60 years starting in 1922. Throughout Prohibition, his speakeasy stashed homemade booze in a secret room accessible through one of the cupboards in back. The current owners have kept the bar in its original shape and the burgers are still some of the best in the city.

Glance down Mercer Street at Manhattan's former Red Light District. Irish immigrants who moved here in the 1840s after the potato famine couldn't pay their rents, so building owners allowed certain rooms to be used as illicit sexual clubs. Mercer Street alone contained 30 brothels, including the Fanelli Café.

Continue on Prince to Broadway, where you'll notice a Prada store to your left. Designed by Dutch architect Rem Koolhaas, the futuristic store features a concrete half-pipe in its interior, similar to those used by skateboarders, and dressing rooms with one-way glass doors and live-feed video screens instead of mirrors. The building to your immediate right, accommodating Kate's Paperie, is known as the "Little Singer Building." It was built for the Singer Sewing Machine Company in 1904.

Walk up Broadway toward Houston and take in the massive cast iron buildings on your right, and 583 Broadway on your left, built on the site of the house where John Jacob Astor died in 1848. Even though he was the richest man in the country at the time of his death, he famously regretted not purchasing "every foot of land on the island of Manhattan." At the corner of Houston and Broadway you'll see a Crate & Barrel across the street. Designed in 1894 by architect Stanford White, the building is known as the Cable Building. Its basement contained mechanisms for the cable cars that ran along Broadway from 1892 to 1901. At the Cable Building's opposite corner stands one of the best-known independent film houses in New York City, the Angelika Film Center.

Turn right on Houston and walk toward the red Puck Building on Lafayette Street, the front of which was displayed as Grace's interior design office on the television show *Will & Grace*. Built in 1886, the building is named for the statuette of Shakespeare's Puck gracing the façade.

Turn right at Mulberry Street one block down. Jersey Street in the middle of the road doesn't seem to lead anywhere other than a small cemetery. However, this cemetery and the surrounding church buildings are all part of the **Old St. Patrick Cathedral** complex, which extends to the end of this block. Note also the nineteenth-century row houses that have been preserved across the street. Make a left on Prince and another left on Mott to get to the front of the cathedral, which is surrounded by a brick wall built to discourage fighting between Protestants and Catholics. Across the street from the main entrance is an 1888 red brick Children's Aid Society building, designed in part by Central Park architect Calvert Vaux. Real-estate millionaire John Jacob Astor III donated the building in memory of his wife, Charlotte, who encouraged Astor to contribute to women's and children's hospitals.

Once back on Prince, head back toward Broadway, turning left on Crosby. Crosby Street is hidden between the more populated streets in this neighborhood, and the cobblestone keeps cars and bicyclists away. Continue down to Broome and turn right, passing the OK Hardware Store on your right. If you're with a child or easily amused friend, pick up a magnet to locate the cast iron buildings in the neighborhood. Only true cast iron structures are magnetic. The Staples store on the corner of Broadway sits in one of the most significant cast iron constructions in the city. Known as the E. V. Haughwout Building, this 1857 silver, china, and crystal store supplied the Lincoln White House with dinnerware and had the first commercial elevator in a retail space. The building has been called the "Parthenon of cast iron architecture," in part because of the cast iron panels on two of its sides. A clock appropriately graces the entrance, since clocks were one of the items Eder V. Haughwout sold here back in the day. If Astor's regret about not buying more Manhattan real estate has inspired you to purchase a pied-à-terre in SoHo, the Corcoran Group's downtown real-estate offices are conveniently located upstairs. Across the street, the New Era Building has an imaginative copper roof, which is unfortunately difficult to see from the street.

Stay on Broome until you get to Greene Street. The Gunther Building on the southwest corner of Greene Street is named after furrier William H. Gunther, who commissioned the space as a warehouse in the 1870s. Continuing down Greene past Grand, 28–30 Greene Street on your left is known as the "Queen of Greene Street" because of the beauty of its cast iron architecture. Notice how the windows are reduced at each level, giving the building greater stature. Crossing Canal Street, veer right toward the post office so that you end up on Church Street.

Once south of Canal, you are officially in Tribeca. As you walk down Church, you'll see the back of the massive AT&T Long Lines Building. Built in 1974 as a telecom equipment tower, the nearly windowless structure was designed to defend light-sensitive equipment against nuclear disasters. Each floor in the building is eighteen feet high, twice the height of a standard New York floor, and the building has enough provisions to sustain itself for two weeks in the case of a homeland emergency.

Turn right on White Street and cross the street, passing the clock that stands in front of the Tribeca Grand Hotel. Completed in 2000, the hotel is busiest during the Tribeca Film Festival in the spring. In keeping with its industry clientele, the hotel has a private screening room and offers guests compli- mentary goldfish upon request.

Turn left on West Broadway and right onto Franklin. Glance diagonally at the northwest corner of Franklin and Hudson, where you'll see the 1892 Powell Building, built by Carrere & Hastings, the same architects who designed the New York Public Library. Walk down Hudson, where you'll see the New York Mercantile Exchange Building on Hudson and Harrison. The NYMEX was founded in 1872 as the Butter and Cheese Exchange, and the high second-story windows once illuminated its trading floor. Puffy's Tavern on the corner is a Prohibition-era watering hole with its original bar and tile floor.

Turn right on Harrison and notice the preserved early-nineteenth-century Federal houses near Greenwich Street. Find Staple Street midway down the block and turn onto it, glancing to your left at the enormous Western Union Building on Hudson. If you look closely, you'll see the nineteen shades of brick that art deco architect Ralph Walker used to lighten the building as it fades into the sky. You'll also see an undulating pattern in the brick on the first setback, evoking sound waves, which is fitting for a telegraph, telephone, and ticker machine company. If you have a moment, run over and glance at the landmarked art deco lobby before continuing on.

Stay on Staple Street until you get to Duane Street and Duane Park, purchased in 1797 as the first public parkland in the city. Walk west on Duane toward Greenwich Street, where you'll see Washington Market Park, formerly the site of the city's wholesale produce center. Continue down Greenwich to Chambers Street and turn right, following Chambers to West Street. You'll pass the campus of Borough of Manhattan Community College. At West Street, ascend the steps to the Tribeca Bridge and walk across it (or simply walk across West Street if the bridge is closed). An entrance to **Stuyvesant High School** is immediately in front of you. Follow the sign to Roosevelt Park to your left, and at the base of the stairs continue down Chambers Street toward the Hudson River. You'll pass Stuyvesant's main entrance on your right. As you continue toward the water you'll see steps leading into Roosevelt Park. Stop here to rest and enjoy the view or walk along the water to explore **Battery Park City**.

The Ear Inn

The Ear Inn, or James Brown House, as it is officially known, was once five feet from New York's original shoreline. James Brown, a black aide to George Washington during the Revolutionary War, built the house in 1817 with money made in the tobacco trade. After Brown sold it, the house was used as a spiritual establishment, and then later as a brewery for thirsty sailors. By around 1900, the brewery became a restaurant, with the present-day dining room constructed from a former backyard and garden. The house served as a speakeasy during Prohibition, with, consecutively, a boarding house, smugglers' den, and brothel upstairs. The bar lost its name during Prohibition and for years was simply known as "the Green Door" by the seamen who frequented it as a clubhouse. In 1977, new resident owners changed the "B" of Bar to an "E" for Ear to avoid waiting for city approval of a new sign. Only a handful of Federal houses are left in the city, and this is one of the best preserved. The bottles above the bar were all dug out of the basement below the dining room, and maps, posters, and portraits from an earlier time adorn the walls.

Cast Iron District

Cast iron architecture was very popular starting in the late 1850s. This innovation enabled the construction of grand building façades with relatively little effort. The process itself involved the use of ready-made frames for a building's exterior, the strength of which accommodated elaborate design elements such as large window spans and classical columns and arches, and the lightness of which made for easy maneuverability. Cast iron exteriors were mass generated and conveniently available to developers through catalogs. Because of its speed, versatility, and cost-efficiency, cast iron was the ideal material for the commercial buildings that once dominated this neighborhood. Today SoHo has the largest and most outstanding concentration of cast iron buildings in the world. Most of the buildings you see were constructed during the golden age of cast iron architecture, which lasted from 1855 to 1885.

Old St. Patrick Cathedral

In 1815, when Old St. Patrick Cathedral was completed, the Catholic population of New York numbered 16,000, but there was only one church for worship downtown. Since that time, the cathedral has served generations of Catholic immigrants in America, including the Irish, German, French, and Italian communities in the area. The 1852 organ is still used in present-day liturgies, and is one of less than a dozen of its kind surviving in New York

today. A labyrinth of mortuary vaults exists underneath the church, and next door an old cemetery contains the graves of prominent Catholics, including Pierre Toussaint, a Haitian former slave who used money from his hairdressing business to buy the freedom of other slaves. The seat of the Archdiocese of New York moved to St. Patrick's Cathedral on Fifth Avenue and 50th Street when it was completed in 1879, and today Old St. Patrick Cathedral is a parish church serving mostly the neighborhood Italian- and Dominican-American communities.

Stuyvesant High School

Named for Dutch colonial governor Peter Stuyvesant, this high school was founded as a "manual training school for boys" with an emphasis on math, science, and technology. Initially a school for immigrants, half of its student body still consists of first- or second-generation Americans and includes native speakers of almost every language in the world. Stuyvesant has always been tuition free, but every prospective student has to take a standardized exam that only four percent of applicants pass. Among Stuyvesant distinguished alumni are three Nobel Prize laureates, jazz musician Thelonius Monk, and actor James Cagney. Additionally, author Frank McCourt taught creative writing here before writing Angela's Ashes. The school building on Chambers Street was completed in 1992. Until that time, the school was located on 15th Street near the East River.

Battery Park City

In the 1960s, the initial plan for Battery Park City proposed a futuristic community with pedestrian traffic on one level and transportation on a subterranean level. By the late 1970s, the master plan was reworked to combine Manhattan's traditional street grid with new parks and public spaces. Battery Park City is considered an achievement in urban planning not only for its fusion of urban practicality and park aesthetic, but also for its commitment to ecological responsibility. The Solaire on the north end of the park is the first "green" residential building in the country, designed to conserve natural resources. At its southernmost tip, the promenade contains the Museum of Jewish Heritage and the Skyscraper Museum. In the summer, the River-to-River Festival features free live musical performances, lectures, and cultural events. Since its conception, public art has been an important part of the park's design, so look out for a wide range of sculptures along your stroll.

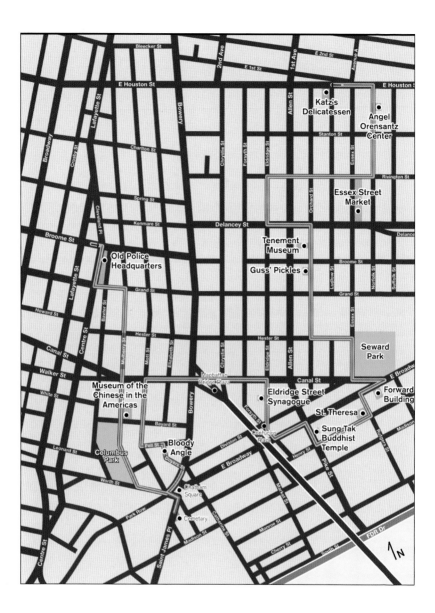

Lower East Side

T he ethnically diverse character of New York City is no longer confined to the Lower East Side, but in 1910 this neighborhood contained 400,000 inhabitants per square mile, a higher density of people than any other city in the world. Back then, peddlers pushed carts through the streets, selling everything from fabric to milk, local theaters provided provincial entertainment, and turf wars erupted between rival gangs. Temples, cafés, and even dry-goods stores served as community centers for immigrants, providing post offices, news and bank services, and venues for social contact.

Little Italy, Chinatown, and the Jewish Lower East Side used to be distinct neighborhoods, but the ethnic sections of the city have merged and now former churches are Buddhist temples, former synagogues are Catholic churches, and different languages share the same awning. Although the immigrants that arrived on boats settled in Manhattan, immigrants that came after the 1950s and 1960s moved to Queens near John F. Kennedy Airport, and Queens has come to surpass Manhattan as the new ethnic center of the city. However, the Lower East Side retains much of its Old World spirit, culture, and cuisine, and a walk through this part of town offers unique insight into the city's varied heritage.

Start:	Broome Street between Centre Street and Cleveland Place
Finish:	Houston and Ludlow Street
Length:	2 miles
Time:	2 hours

Refreshments: Umberto's Clamhouse for authentic Italian, Sweet-n-Tart Restaurant for Dim Sum, Schiller's Liquor Bar for late afternoon snacks like calamari, steak frites, or mac 'n' cheese, and Katz's Delicatessen for the best pastrami sandwich in the city.

Sights: Old Police Headquarters Building, Little Italy, Franciscan Fathers Church of the Most Precious Blood, Chinatown, Museum of the Chinese in the Americas, Chatham Square, Confucius Plaza, "Bloody Angle," Church of the Transfiguration, Jewish Lower East Side, Eldridge Street Synagogue, Forward Building, Streit's Matzo, Angel Orensanz Center, Katz's Delicatessen.

The **Old Police Headquarters Building** on Broome between Centre Street and Cleveland Place is hard to miss. One block east is Umberto's Clamhouse, where in 1972 the gangster Joey Gallo was shot and killed during a family dinner. Stay on Cleveland Place heading downtown. You'll notice awnings with Chinese lettering on your right, indicating your proximity to Chinatown.

Turn left onto Grand Street and walk east past O'Neal's Grand Street Bar, a former saloon and brothel for police officers and journalists on the crime beat. A tunnel downstairs once connected the bar to the police station, allowing discretion during Prohibition. You'll come to Mulberry Street, which is the central street of **Little Italy**. Here you'll find Italian specialty stores with some of the best cheeses and cured meats in the city. Ferrara Café on the south side of Grand Street was a gathering place for opera enthusiasts and singers, operated by opera promoter Antonio Ferrara from 1892. The café is still run by Antonio's family.

Head south on Mulberry past the restaurants and gift shops, crossing Hester, and look for Franciscan Fathers Church of the Most Precious Blood on your right, just before Canal Street. This is an example of the many Roman Catholic churches that cropped up along these streets in the early twentieth century when Italian immigrants occupied this section of the city. Inside stands the statue of San Gennaro, which is carried through the streets during the September Feast of San Gennaro.

Cross Canal Street into **Chinatown**, and you'll see a red information kiosk down the street to your right. As you make your way down Mulberry, you'll see a number of outdoor markets featuring live and cooked Chinese delicacies, as well as household appliances and tableware, and Chinese fruits and vegetables. At Bayard Street you'll come to the Museum of the Chinese in the Americas on your left, dedicated to preserving and interpreting the Chinese immigrant experience in the United States. As you continue down Mulberry, you'll see Columbus Park, once the seediest slum in the city, now filled with neighborhood school children on weekday afternoons. Back when this was Little Italy, the street used to be referred to as "Death Row" for the funeral homes on your left.

Turn left on Worth and cross Mott Street heading toward Chatham Square, once the center for horse auctions. This area is also known as Kimlau Square, for Chinese-American World War II hero Benjamin Kimlau, who is immortalized along with all Chinese-American soldiers who fought for the United States by the granite arch. In the mid-1800s, this part of the city was cramped with brothels, saloons, and tattoo parlors. By the 1930s, Prohibition and the Great Depression led to its crackdown and later resurgence. The Lin Ze Xu monument nearby depicts the Qing

(Ch'ing) dynasty official who helped stop the opium invasion of China in 1839.

Several streets branch off from Chatham Square. Find St. James Place to the south of the square, and walk midway down the block, looking for a cemetery on your left. This cemetery, dating back to 1683, is the First Cemetery of the Shearith Israel congregation, the only Jewish congregation in New York from 1654 to 1825.

Make your way back to Chatham Square and head toward Catherine Street. On the corner of Division Street is **Confucius Plaza**, featuring a statue honoring the Chinese philosopher in front of a high-rise development. Look for the Chase Bank to your left on Doyers Street and follow its curve. The United States Postal Service building was a bar where fledgling singers including Irving Berlin got their start. Legend has it that the street was originally built at an angle to throw off straight-flying ghosts. Around 1900, it was known as "Bloody Angle" for the Chinese gang wars that took place here. On early mornings local shopkeepers mopped up the river of blood that flowed onto Bowery Street. Nam Wah Tea Parlor on your left, dating back to 1920, is the oldest Chinese tea parlor in Chinatown. At the end of the bend is Pell Street, also known as "Haircut Street," because of the number of barber and beauty shops.

Turn left on Pell to get to Mott Street. Directly across the street, you'll see the **Church of the Transfiguration**, built in 1801. Good Fortune Gifts to your left is the oldest dry-goods store in the neighborhood. Walk against the traffic on Mott Street until you get back on Canal, and turn right. The former Citizens' Savings Bank building on the corner of Bowery was once the site of the Bull's Head Tavern, where George Washington marched triumphantly into the city after the British evacuated on November 25, 1783.

Cross Canal, and then Bowery to the east, heading toward the Mahayana Buddhist Temple, the largest

Buddhist temple in Chinatown. The 1916 Manhattan Bridge Plaza directly ahead of you was built by New York Public Library architects Carrere and Hastings as a commanding entrance to Manhattan from Brooklyn.

Stay on Canal, passing a playground on your left, until you get to Eldridge Street, one of the main streets of the **Jewish Lower East Side**. Turn right on Eldridge and you'll see the **Eldridge Street Synagogue** on your left down the block. Tours of the temple are offered several days a week. The buses on Forsythe Street are the cheapest way to get to Boston, Philadelphia, or Washington, DC from Manhattan.

Follow Forsythe to East Broadway, home to the Fujianese population from China's southeastern coast, and turn left. Turn right onto Pike Street where you'll see Sung Tak Buddhist Temple, a former synagogue, in a building constructed in 1903. At Henry Street, turn left and walk half a block to Rutgers Street. St. Teresa Catholic Church was a Presbyterian church built in 1841 that has been used as a Catholic church since 1863. Today, masses are held in English, Spanish, and Chinese.

Follow Rutgers to East Broadway and cross over to Straus Square. The tallest building you can see on East Broadway is the Forward Building. The *Jewish Daily Forward* Yiddish-language newspaper was started here in 1897, at one point reaching a readership of 250,000. The playground on the other side of Straus Square is part of Seward Park. Cross over to it and follow Essex Street uptown to Hester Street. While walking on Hester, observe how antiquated neighborhood spots like kosher Gertel's Bakery Luncheon, serving Jewish treats like rugelach and potato kugel, stand side by side with the trendy eateries of the Lower East Side. On Hester Street between Ludlow and Orchard you'll see a beautiful public school on your right, built in 1898. Farther down the block was an area derogatorily referred to as the "pig market," where immigrant garment workers, who worked in sweatshops and were paid by the piece, gathered to negotiate employment.

Turn up Orchard, and after you pass Grand Street, look for Guss's Pickles on your left, founded by Russian immigrant Izzy Guss in 1920. The Lower East Side Tenement Museum Store is on the corner of Broome, and across the exposed brick of Orchard Street is 97 Orchard, a preserved tenement house used in museum tours. The museum's visitors' center is located beneath Joe's Fabrics and Trimmings, on the corner of Delancey.

Turn left on Delancey and cross over to Allen Street. The public restrooms that sit in the middle of the street were built for tenement dwellers who lacked indoor plumbing. The Church of Grace to Fujianese north of Allen Street is a former bathhouse that was built for the same purpose.

Continue on Delancey and turn up Eldridge, walking past the third home of the New York Chinese Alliance Church, formed in 1971. At 184 Eldridge Street on the corner of Rivington, you'll see the University Settlement. Founded in 1886 as a neighborhood haven for new immigrants, this is the oldest settlement house in the country. Turn right to see an old synagogue across the street, built in 1903 for a Romanian Jewish congregation. The space has served as artists' studios and residences since the 1970s.

Stay on Rivington until you pass Orchard Street again, where you'll see the First Romanian-American Congregation on your right. This former German Evangelical Church was built in 1850, bought by the Romanian congregation Shaaray Hashamoyim ("gates of the heavens") in 1864, turned into a Methodist church in 1890, and then into a Romanian temple again in 1902. The synagogue was known as the "Cantor's Carnegie Hall" for its cantors, who went on to become successful opera singers. Directly across the street is musician Moby's vegan tearoom.

Cross Ludlow and look out for Economy Candy on your left. One of the most impressively stocked candy stores in the city, the place has been run by the

Cohen family since 1937. The contemporary glass structure across the street is the Hotel on Rivington. Completed in 2004, amenities in the "Unique" set of rooms include a three-person steam shower, while the "Owner's Suite" offers a separate bedroom with bunk beds, each equipped with its own flat-screen TV. Look to your right on Essex and you'll see the Essex Street Market. In the 1930s Mayor Fiorello LaGuardia founded the market as a permanent home for pushcart vendors. Today the market is stocked with meat, produce, and other food retailers, as well as a barber, tailor, and television repair shop.

Continue past Essex—where you'll see Sugar Sweet Sunshine Bakery on your left, with some of the tastiest cupcakes in New York, and Rivington Guitars on your right, selling some of the best vintage guitars and equipment—and then turn up Norfolk Street. Beyond the basketball courts you'll see a sign for Streit's. This matzo company has been making unleavened bread and other kosher food used during the Jewish Passover holiday since 1925, and has been family run since Aron and Nettie Streit opened it five generations ago.

Walk past Stanton Street and you'll see a bright red building that looks like a house of worship. Spanish-born sculptor Angel Orensanz purchased this

1849 synagogue for use as a studio in 1986. He then turned the space into a cultural center, offering talks, art programs, and performances.

Turn left on East Houston and walk toward Ludlow Street. You'll pass the Mercury Lounge on your left, one of the city's eminent punk, rock, and alternative live music venues, whose past performers have included Joan Jett, Lou Reed, Jeff Buckley, Squeeze, and Radiohead. On the corner of Houston and Ludlow you'll find Katz's Delicatessen. This Jewish deli, dating back to 1888, has the best pastrami in the city, as well as excellent frankfurters, potato pancakes, matzo ball soup, and cold cuts. Although the dining experience can be transcendent (as Meg Ryan demonstrated in the romantic comedy *When Harry Met Sally*), it is not particularly user friendly, so just remember to hold onto your ticket until you've paid. The walls are lined with photos of brother-in-law owners Fred Austin and Alan Dell posing with celebrities who have dined here.

On a rainy day, head to Landmark's Sunshine Cinema three blocks west. The 1840s Dutch church housed both a boxing venue and a Yiddish vaudeville theater before it became a movie theater showing art-house films on five screens.

OLD POLICE HEADQUARTERS BUILDING

From 1909 to 1973, this French Renaissance-style building is where the New York Police Department brought criminals "downtown." Strategically situated near the former Five Points slum four blocks south, many notorious New York City felons have been booked, fingerprinted, and interrogated here. Among the police commissioners that have served here was former President Theodore Roosevelt. In 1987 the building was converted into luxury apartments, and supermodels Cindy Crawford, Naomi Campbell, and Linda Evangelista all lived here, as well as fashion designer Calvin Klein. Today you will notice that

uniformed police officers still have the number 3100 on their badges, which is the building's old telephone exchange number.

LITTLE ITALY

The oldest ethnic district in New York was born in the 1850s when Italian immigrants moved into the neighborhood later to be known as Little Italy. For about a century, the streets were filled with bocce ball games, homemade gelato, and the scent of Italian cooking, while family and friends lived within earshot. Yet even within this cloistered community, subgroups kept their distance. Genoans, Calabrians, and Sicilians lived in certain areas, while Piedmontese, Tuscans, and Neapolitans lived in others. The neighborhood once extended as far south as present-day Chinatown and as far north as SoHo, but today Mulberry Street is the only part that has been preserved, and it is illegal to have non-English writing on the awnings of the two blocks north of Canal Street. As is evident by the numerous souvenir shops selling Italian flags, gangster movie stills, T-shirts, and bumper stickers, the neighborhood has become more of a tourist attraction than the center of the Italian community.

CHINATOWN

A handful of Chinese immigrated to the United States starting in 1784, most of whom were sailors. In the 1840s Chinese laborers came to California to capitalize on the gold rush and the construction of the transcontinental railroad, but moved east by the 1870s to escape the vicious anti-Chinese sentiment of white laborers who resented the cheap workforce. The 1882 Chinese Exclusion Act prevented these immigrants

from attaining citizenship, and also prohibited wives and families from joining their husbands, leading to a "bachelor society" with a static population. Popular jobs for immigrants included laundry service, which required little financing or language skills, and the restaurant industry, which prompted tourism. Temples and Chinese organizations such as tongs served as internal governing structures, but violent tong wars between the On Leong and Hip Sing lasted until 1924. The Chinese Exclusion Act was lifted in 1943 and the community grew incrementally until 1968, when immigration quotas were abolished altogether, and the Chinese population in the country exploded. By this point, newer immigrants moved to the outer boroughs such as Flushing, Queens, which boasts the largest and wealthiest Chinatown in the country. Manhattan's Chinatown is not restricted to Chinese inhabitants, but also includes immigrants from other Asian as well as Latin American countries.

Confucius Plaza

The Confucius statue was a gift from the Chinese Consolidated Benevolent Association to the city in 1976 to celebrate the country's bicentennial. Beneath the Confucius monument is a Roman inscription of Confucius's utopian age of Great Harmony, in which the philosopher postulates a structured and compassionate society. In 1974, the Confucius Plaza high-rise developers, who built the large buildings behind the monument, refused to hire Chinese laborers, claiming that they weren't strong enough for construction work. The group Asian Americans for Equality (AAFE) was formed, and they led the community in protest against the construction firm's discriminatory practices. Black and Latino construction workers joined the movement as well, and ultimately 27 minority workers were hired, many of whom were Asian.

Church of the Transfiguration

This church is a prime example of the cultural mix that defines the Lower East Side. Originally an English Lutheran church, the building was bought by Roman Catholics in the 1850s. Italians worshipped in the basement while Irish worshipped on the ground floor, but in time, Italians moved to the ground floor and a Chinese congregation worshipped in the basement. Today services are offered in English, Mandarin, and Cantonese. The bronze plaque on the church's exterior lists Irish and Italian soldiers who died in World War I.

Jewish Lower East Side

Starting in 1880, well over a million Eastern European Jews immigrated to the United States to escape religious persecution, and by 1910 the Jews that settled in New York ended up accounting for 25 percent of the city's population. Most of these immigrants moved to the Lower East Side, where they lived in five-story tenement buildings intended for single families but inhabited by 20 families or more. The living conditions were overcrowded and unsanitary, and even the airshafts of dumbbell buildings (which gave them their dumbbell shapes) were mostly used as dumping grounds for garbage. Despite the dismal conditions, immigrants worked in the garment and tobacco industries as well as construction, at first pushing carts on the street but ultimately starting family businesses that would last for generations. The community also produced star entertainers such as Jimmy Durante and Benny Goodman, and radical political activists such as Abe Cahan and Emma Goldman. Like most of the other ethnic groups that once resided on the Lower East Side, the religious Jewish community has since moved out of this area and into the outer boroughs.

ELDRIDGE STREET SYNAGOGUE

In 1887, this synagogue was the first for Eastern European Jews, from whom 80 percent of American Jews descend. The founding members were a group of Russian Jews who had settled here as early as the 1850s, and so were able to contribute to this prominent house

of worship for the community. By the beginning of the twentieth century as many as 1,000 worshippers attended services here. During the High Holidays in the fall, police officers on horseback were sent to keep order in the streets. If you get a chance to glance inside, look for the ark where Torah scrolls were stored, facing Jerusalem to the west. You'll also see the *bimah*, or platform where the Torah is read, symbolic of the sacrificial altars of biblical temples. Because it is an orthodox synagogue, women and men sit separately, the women on the balcony level and the men on the ground level.

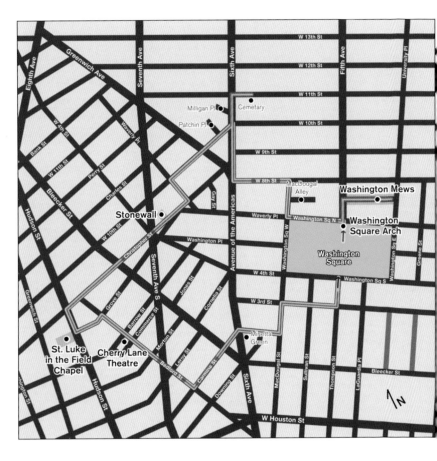

Greenwich Village

"The Village" is a time capsule of old New York, salvaged from an era before the logic of grids and the immensity of vertical towers. A former marshland, the area only became heavily populated between the years 1825 and 1840 due to a series of cholera and yellow fever outbreaks downtown. Throughout the nineteenth century, the neighborhood developed into a cultural and ultimately counter-cultural center of art studios, small presses, and experimental theater companies, but an increase in real-estate prices led to current residents who are more likely to work in investment banks than spend their days writing in outdoor cafés.

Nevertheless, the sun shines differently in the village, as is evident by the tucked-away houses and winding roads that twinkle with the secret history of old New York. So hidden are these streets from the rest of the city that any new bar scene, artistic initiative, or social movement is allowed to flourish here away from the public eye before entering mainstream life. Perhaps this is why the village is known for its literary haunts and gay subculture, its community of freed slaves and anti-establishment art circle, its hidden speakeasies and whimsical gardens you might never find if you don't know where to look.

The Greenwich Village Walk

Start:	Fifth Avenue and Washington Square Park North
Finish:	Thompson and Washington Square Park South
Length:	1.5 miles
Time:	1.5 hours

Refreshments: The French Roast for 24-hour omelets, Gray's Papaya for authentic New York hot dogs, Grey Dog Café for salads and sandwiches, Joe's Pizza for the best pizza in Greenwich Village, Jane for casual American.

Sights: Washington Square Arch, Washington Mews, Mac-Dougal Alley, Milligan Place, Jefferson Market Courthouse, Patchin Place, Northern Dispensary, Stonewall Bistro, St. Luke in the Field Chapel, Grove Court, Chumley's, Cherry Lane Theatre, Isaacs-Hendricks House, Edna St. Vincent Millay Doll House, Minetta Tavern.

Originally a graveyard for criminals, prostitutes, and slaves, Washington Square Park has also served as a drill ground for Revolutionary troops and a site for public executions. The **Washington Square Arch** stands at the north end of the park, and if you stand in the middle of it, you'll see the cars on Fifth Avenue coming straight at you before sharply turning to either side. When Fifth Avenue was a two-way street in the 1930s, the middle of this arch was a traffic circle that looped around the fountain. Robert Moses wanted to extend Fifth Avenue through Washington Square, but American First Lady and Greenwich Village hero Eleanor Roosevelt prevented the extension, and even managed to turn Fifth Avenue into the one-way street it is today.

The creation of Washington Square in the 1820s led to the construction of the row of houses along the northern end of the park, which still retain their original glory. 7 Washington Square North was the home of Alexander Hamilton and later Jon Taylor Johnson, whose son Jon Taylor Johnson, Jr. became the first president of the Metropolitan Museum of Art in 1870. Johnson, Sr., sold the building to a twenty-year-old Edith Wharton, who lived here with her mother in 1882. Edward and Jo Hopper lived on the top floor of 3 Washington Square North from 1913 until the artist's death in 1967. Architect Richard Morris Hunt, who designed Carnegie Hall, the Metropolitan Museum of Art, and the foundation of the Statue of Liberty, lived in 2 Washington Square North from 1887 to 1895. Today New York University, founded in 1831, owns all of the buildings surrounding Washington Square Park and students use the park as their quadrangle.

Cross Washington Square North heading up Fifth Avenue and on your right you'll see the Lewis and Loretta Glucksman Ireland House, NYU's Irish studies center. If you make an immediate right after this building you'll see the **Washington Mews**, the gates of which are always open to pedestrians. Walk through the Mews, then retrace your steps back to park and walk to the northwest corner of Washington Square. The enormous tree to your left is the elm from which executed criminals were allegedly hanged. Gallows were more likely used for hanging, but the tree dates back to the seventeenth century, making it possibly the oldest tree in Manhattan. Across the street from this tree to the west is 29 Washington Square West. Eleanor Roosevelt moved here in 1945 after her husband's death, but abruptly moved out of the building in 1949 when its staff asked her African-American dinner party guests to enter through the service entrance. She soon relocated to the East Village.

Head north on Washington Square West until you see a sign for MacDougal Alley to your left. Built in the 1830s as stables for wealthy Washington Square residents, the houses in MacDougal Alley served as artists' studios by the early 1900s. 19 MacDougal Alley is where Whitney Museum of American Art founder Gertrude Vanderbilt Whitney started her studio. Unfortunately, the gate to this alley is usually locked. Make a left on 8th Street and a right onto Sixth Avenue. Gray's Papaya on the corner, with its famous New York hot dogs and papaya juice, has been serving New Yorkers for over 30 years. The papaya juice supposedly cures all ills.

Walk up Sixth Avenue until you get to 11th Street and make a right. You'll see a small triangular cemetery on your right called the Second Cemetery of Spanish-Portuguese Synagogue, where Jews of Spanish and

Portuguese descent were buried from 1805 to 1829. Walk back to Sixth, cross the avenue and turn left. Mid-block, between 10th and 11th Streets on your right-hand side, is Milligan Place. This former property of Samuel Milligan, who bought the farmland in 1799, features 1850s-era boarding houses that accommodated employees of local businesses. At 10th Street you'll see the large Victorian Gothic structure of the **Jefferson Market Courthouse**.

Make a right on 10th Street and you'll see Patchin Place. Aaron Patchin was Samuel Milligan's (of Milligan Place) land surveyor and, after he married Milligan's daughter Isobel, his son-in-law as well. Patchin built these houses in 1848, which served as domestic servants' quarters, but E. E. Cummings, Ezra Pound, and Marlon Brando all lived here at various times. The street lamp was New York's last functioning gas lamp, but has since been electrified. The iron gates are usually unlocked, so feel free to wander in and look around.

Continuing along 10th Street, you have a beautiful view of the Jefferson Market garden on your left. At Waverly Place, turn left and walk straight until you come to an oddly shaped building that says Northern Dispensary. The Dispensary provided healthcare for yellow-fever victims in the 1920s, and Edgar Allan Poe was treated for a cold here in 1936.

On Stonewall Place where you are now standing, walk toward Seventh Avenue. You'll see the brick **Stonewall Bistro** on your right. Across from the bar is Christopher Park, which contains life-sized sculptures of gay and lesbian couples designed by George Segal and entitled "Gay Liberation." These sculptures, created to promote tolerance, stand paradoxically near a statue of Philip Henry Sheridan, who famously stated, "The only good Indian is a dead Indian." On Seventh Avenue, notice the flat-faced buildings whose corners got sliced off when the city extended the Seventh Avenue subway from 12th Street to Houston Street in 1914.

Cross the avenue and walk a block south so that you're on the corner of Seventh and Christopher Street in front of Village Cigars. In the 1910s, the Hess family placed a triangular mosaic in front of the door to protest the appropriation of their land for Seventh Avenue. When Village Cigars moved here in 1922, they bought the tiny mosaic from the Hess family for $1,000. Continue west on Christopher until you get to Hudson Street, at which point turn left. Once you see Grove, cross Hudson to **St. Luke in the Field**

Chapel. Feel free to wander into the rose garden adjoining the church if it's open.

Cross back over to Grove and follow it east to Bedford Street. On your right you'll pass Grove Court, a small private court created in 1848. Nicknamed "Mixed Ale Alley," a Grove Street grocer named Samuel Cocks built the court to supply housing for working-class customers of his grocery store. The design of the court was novel for its time because the buildings don't face the street. The area inspired O Henry's story "The Last Leaf," and it was used in the 1952 movie *O Henry's Full House*. If you were to continue down Grove you'd come to 59 Grove, now Marie's Crisis Café, where Thomas Paine, author of "The Age of Reason" died alone in the back of the house. The café is named after Paine's 1776 pamphlet "The Crisis" and a plaque on the building commemorates the author. At night Marie's is a lively piano bar. Bedford is one of the earliest recorded streets in the village, named after Bedford Street in London. Turn right onto Bedford and look for 86 Bedford on your left. The unmarked door dating back to the 1830s is the entrance to the former speakeasy, **Chumley's**. The next street you'll pass is Barrow, named after Thomas Barrow. Barrow Street used to be called Reason Street in honor of Paine, but the city renamed it once they realized that people were pronouncing it "Raisin."

Make a right at Commerce and you'll see the **Cherry Lane Theatre**. Next door, 48 Commerce is a landmark house from 1844. Back on Bedford you'll see 77 Bedford on the southwest corner, and 75 1/2 Bedford next door. Built in 1799, 77 Bedford is the oldest house in the village. It is called the Isaacs-Hendricks House after its original owner, copper merchant Harmon Hendricks. 75 1/2 Bedford is the narrowest house in New York. It is known as the Edna St. Vincent Millay Doll House after the poet, who lived here from 1892 to 1950. During prohibition, Edna and her sister Norma tended bar for Lee Chumley across the street.

Continue along Bedford until you get to Carmine and turn left. Walk all the way across Sixth Avenue until you reach Minetta Lane. Minetta Green to your right is a .056 acre memorial to a trout brook that ran from Gramercy Park to West Houston, where it emptied into the Hudson River. Native Americans told the Dutch about this brook in the 1620s, referring to it as "Mannette," or "Devil's Water." As early as the 1640s, freed slaves and their families settled along Minetta Brook, and by the nineteenth century the area was known as "Little Africa" because of all of its black residents. Farther down Minetta Lane on the corner of MacDougal Street is the **Minetta Tavern**.

Make a left on MacDougal and you'll see 130–132 MacDougal Street on your right. Louisa May Alcott wrote *Little Women* here in the 1860s. Turn right on West 3rd Street and you'll see New York University Law School on your right. In the middle of the next block (between Sullivan and Thompson), you'll see 85 West 3rd Street on your left. Writer Edgar Allan Poe resided here from 1845 to 1846. A left on Thompson will lead you back to Washington Square Park.

Washington Square Arch

The original Washington Square Arch was a wood and plaster tribute to George Washington, erected on the centennial of his inauguration in 1889. In 1895,

wealthy residents of Washington Square North commissioned famed architect Stanford White to design a permanent white marble fixture that would rival those of European capitals. The east side of the arch, designed by Henry MacNeil, features Washington at war accompanied by Fame and Valor; the west side features Washington in peace, accompanied by Wisdom and Justice, and was designed by Alexander Stirling Calder (mobile artist Alexander Calder's dad). In January 1917, a group of antiwar radicals, anticipating the country's imminent involvement in World War I, allegedly climbed the inside steps of the arch to the roof and declared themselves the "Free and Independent Republic of Washington Square." The papers referred to this gang as the "New Bohemians," the most famous of whom were artists Marcel Duchamp and John Sloan.

Washington Mews

This alley has remained intact for the past hundred years, but if you look to the west you'll see tall buildings where the alley had once continued on the other side. The south side of the alley served as housing for the domestic servants of park residents, while the north side served as carriage houses. As you can see by the oversized doors, carriages were kept on the ground floor and hay was stored on top. By 1916, with the popularization of the automobile, there was no longer a need for carriages or haylofts, so owners kept their cars downstairs and rented the undesirable upstairs spaces to artists. These artists were referred to disdainfully as the "Ashcan" school of art, because their subject matter was so dark and gritty compared to the dominant style of the day that they might as well have been painting ash cans.

The one wealthy sculptor who was a huge fan of the Ashcan school was Commodore Cornelius Vanderbilt's granddaughter Gertrude Vanderbilt Whitney. Whitney invested in more than $5 million

worth of American art by such painters as Hopper, Sloan, and Prendergast, who all lived in the area, and she also financially supported many of these artists by paying their rent. In 1929 she offered her sizable art collection to John Taylor Johnson, Jr. as a gift to the Metropolitan Museum of Art, but he declined, prompting Whitney to start her own museum, the Whitney Museum of American Art. The museum has grown substantially since the days of Whitney's Greenwich Village studio and it is now a preeminent contemporary art museum on the Upper East Side. As you stroll through the Mews, note the brick roadwork that has endured since the 1800s.

JEFFERSON MARKET COURTHOUSE

Originally a food market and now a branch of the New York Public Library, this 1876 Bavarian castle design was named one of the ten most beautiful buildings in the country in 1885. The courthouse is most famous for the trial of the "murder of the century" in 1906, in

which the eccentric millionaire Harry K. Thaw murdered Stanford White, the most distinguished architect of his day (designer of Washington Square Arch and Madison Square Garden, among other landmarks). Thaw and White ran in the same circles but were not particularly fond of each other, so when White starting seeing a sixteen-year-old chorus girl by the name of Evelyn Nesbit, Thaw set about courting her by showering her with extravagant gifts and lavish trips until she eventually conceded to his advances. In June 1906, fourteen months after their wedding, Thaw saw White at a rooftop performance at Madison Square Garden and was so tormented by the architect's past relationship with Evelyn that he fired three shots directly into White's head. At first the audience thought it was a practical joke, which were common in high society at the time, but they soon realized that White was in fact dead, murdered in the architectural masterpiece that he himself had built. The press sensationalized the trial, which unfolded in this very courthouse, and Thaw's mother persuaded Evelyn to testify against Stanford White with the promise of a divorce and $1 million compensation. Thaw got off on insanity, setting a precedent for murder trials to come, and while Evelyn received a great deal of exposure at the time, she never saw the money. By the time her stage career simmered down, Thaw was declared sane.

By 1927, the Jefferson Market Courthouse was used solely for the trials of women, many of whom were prostitutes sent to the Women's House of Detention next door. In 1965 feminist writer and anti-pornography activist Andrea Dworkin was taken here after participating in an anti–Vietnam War march in her freshman year at Bennington College. She was subjected to a brutal internal exam by prison doctors, and later publicly recounted her experience in letters to newspapers until she got the government to investigate the prison. In 1973, thanks to her efforts, the city tore the prison down and replaced it with a flower garden in her honor that sits at the foot of the Jefferson Market clock tower on Sixth Avenue.

STONEWALL BISTRO

In the 1950s and '60s, when bars could lose their liquor license for "knowingly" serving homosexuals, it was not uncommon for police to raid bars like Stonewall, only to have the proprietors bribe the officers and the officers return to their precinct to distribute the bribes. Although the bars continued to operate, police arrested handfuls of gay patrons and papers published the names of these men, resulting in the loss of their homes and jobs. The raids usually took place early enough in the evening for the bar to reopen later that night, and only a few men were arrested at a time. But on Friday, June 27, 1969, while emotions were running high from Judy Garland's funeral earlier that day, police decided to raid Stonewall at 1:20AM, its most crowded time.

The night resulted in a turning point for the gay community, becoming the first time a significant group resisted an arrest on the basis of their sexuality. Accounts differ as to how the riot started, but a punch was thrown, which prompted the crowd to fight against the police. The bar soon erupted, and the eight original policemen barricaded themselves inside, fearing for their safety. When backup officers showed up in riot gear, they were supposedly met with a kick line of drag queens. Hours later, 2,000 protestors were battling 400 police officers, and by the third night of rioting the crowd numbered 5,000. These riots catapulted the gay rights movement forward and led to the creation of groups like the Gay Liberation Front (GLF), which took on a national and ultimately global presence. In commemoration of the riots, the GLF organized a march the following June, starting at Central Park and continuing to Stonewall. Somewhere between 5,000 and 10,000 marchers showed up for the first Gay Pride Parade, but in recent years the number has exceeded 400,000.

St. Luke in the Field Chapel

In 1820, a group of New Yorkers moved their families north to fields by the Hudson River to escape a yellow-fever outbreak that was plaguing the city. They built an Episcopal church and named it after the physician evangelist St. Luke. By the 1950s, a playground, school, and garden were added, and in the 1980s the church got involved hands-on with the HIV/AIDS epidemic, marching in the annual Gay Pride Parade and serving Saturday dinner and weekend tea to tens of thousands of members of the local community.

CHUMLEY'S

Leland Chumley, an outspoken organizer of the
socialist labor union the Wobblies, or the Industrial
Workers of the World (IWW), ran a bar and gambling
den here during Prohibition. In time, the space
became a major literary hangout, with such patrons as
Jack Kerouac, Bob Dylan, and F. Scott Fitzgerald,
whose portraits, photos, and book jackets, along with
those of many other famous regulars, cover the walls.
The bar has a back exit, visible from Barrow Street,
through which customers would escape during police
raids, and supposedly the term "86," which means to
get out of an establishment quickly, comes from a code
to customers during prohibition warning that police
were on the way (86 Bedford being the bar's address).
Another secret getaway includes a trapdoor rumored
to have led to the Underground Railroad, which
brought runaway slaves to the black community of
Gay Street. The unmarked tavern still serves food and
drink to those who can find it, starting at 5PM daily.

Cherry Lane Theatre

Cherry Lane Theatre is the oldest continuously running Off-Broadway theater in New York City. It was originally built in 1817 as a farm storage area, and served as a tobacco warehouse and a box factory until it became a theater in 1924. At that time, Pulitzer Prize–winning poet Edna St. Vincent Millay, along with a group of artists and actors, commissioned a set designer to convert the spot into a performance space. The 158 original audience chairs are still here. Edward Albee, Samuel Beckett, and Sam Shepard all showcased their plays in this theater, and Beckett's *Waiting for Godot* premiered here. Even Barbra Streisand started off as a Cherry Lane usher. The name of the theater comes from the cherry-tree-lined cow path that once ran through the farm.

Minetta Tavern

Minetta Tavern started off as "The Black Rabbit," a Prohibition-era speakeasy and literary hangout that catered to such customers as Eugene O'Neill. In 1923, DeWitt Wallace launched *Reader's Digest* in the basement of the bar after every publisher in New York rejected his sample issue. The magazine offered an opportunity for self-improvement to middle-class Americans in a manageable information source, and in seven years the *Digest*'s circulation had reached 216,000. By 1937, The Black Rabbit had changed its name to Minetta Tavern, after the brook that supposedly still runs underneath. The walls are lined with photographs and caricatures of famous patrons.

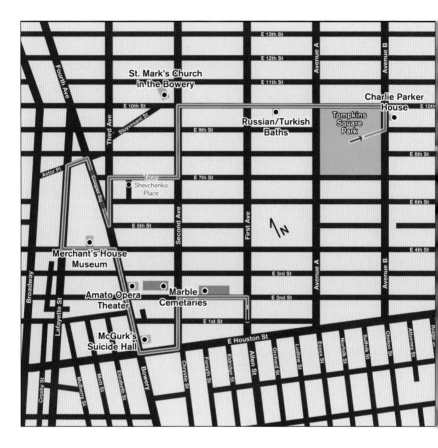

East Village

The history of the East Village is one of a diverse group of thinkers, ranging from eccentric conceptual artists to strong-minded radical idealists to pacifistic followers of Eastern religions. As such, the neighborhood strikes a balance between peaceful cohabitation and perpetual activity, reflected in its abundance of record stores, vegan restaurants, Himalayan craft stores, 24-hour eateries, and live music clubs. Tompkins Square Park, in the middle of the East Village, exemplifies the local temperament as a hub for the diverse groups and individuals that congregate for lively discussion and simple relaxation.

In recent years, real-estate developers have targeted the area, and its trademark gritty streets stand in awkward contrast to the flashy high rises that are being built around them. Nevertheless, the most intriguing part of the East Village has always been the people that live here, and you'll notice their unique style, rarely duplicated in other parts of the city. It is only appropriate, then, that the stores in this part of town cater to experimental designers, the music venues showcase unsigned bands, and many of the bars and restaurants avoid displaying their names to ensure that only locals can find them.

Start at **Tompkins Square Park**, the most prominent greenery in the East Village. In the middle of the park, on the equivalent of 9th Street, is a set of three flags: an American flag, a New York City flag, and a New York City Department of Parks and Recreation flag. To the north of the flags is a playground that contains the **Slocum Memorial Fountain**. To the south, surrounded by gray bricks and wooden benches, is the Hare Krishna elm tree. To the east is a dog run that is considered one of the top five in the country, and just as good for people watching as it is for dog walking. To the west is the Sandra Turner Garden, named for the founder of the East Village Parks Conservancy. Across from the northeast corner of the park on Avenue B is jazz legend Charlie

Parker's house, where he lived from 1950 to 1954. A plaque outside explains the architectural significance of the landmark, as well as the former resident's influence on American jazz.

From the northern boundary of Tompkins Square Park, walk west on 10th Street until you get to Second Avenue. You'll pass the St. Nicholas of Myra Carpatho Russian Orthodox Church on your left, designed by James Renwick, Jr., who also designed St. Patrick's Cathedral on Fifth Avenue, as well as a Turkish bath house that has been offering spa treatments since 1892. The Second Avenue Deli was formerly on the southeast corner of Second Avenue and 10th Street, and was arguably the best kosher deli in New York. To acknowledge what was once a predominantly Jewish part of town, the sidewalk outside displays the names of Yiddish theater luminaries. Diagonally across the street is **St. Mark's Church in the Bowery**, named after Peter Stuyvesant's 1651 farm (from the Dutch word *bowerij*). Second Avenue hosts one of the largest populations of Ukrainians in the United States, and as you make your way south you'll see a number of Ukrainian restaurants, bars, and community centers in this area, such as the Ukrainian National Home and the 24-hour Ukrainian restaurant Veselka, both on the left.

When you get to 8th Street, or "St. Mark's Place," as this part of town is referred, you'll find an area that has gone through incarnations as a jazz, then beat, then punk hangout. With its abundance of sidewalk cafes and street vendors, St. Mark's Place is one of the most vibrant pedestrian areas of Manhattan. Some of the older bars, such as St. Mark's Ale House on Third Avenue, formerly known as "The Five Spot," provided gathering points for musicians and poets in the 1960s.

Continue down Second Avenue and make a right on 7th Street. On the next corner, you'll see another example of the Ukrainian presence in the neighborhood, with Taras Shevchenko Place. Taras Shevchenko (1814–1861) was a Ukranian artist, poet, archeologist, and political theorist. His writing defined Ukrainian modern literature even as its politically subversive content led to his expulsion from the Ukraine. Directly across 7th Street is **McSorley's Old Ale House**, in almost pristine original condition.

A few more steps will bring you to Cooper Square. Walk toward the large brown building that comprises **Cooper Union for the Advancement of Science and Art**. Peter Cooper, an illiterate but successful businessmen and proponent of free education, founded this full-scholarship architecture and engineering college in 1859. Enter the building, the front of which is directly behind the Peter Cooper monument on 7th Street, and you'll see a thank-you note to Peter Cooper from the school's first students in an elaborate wooden frame on the back wall. Ask to go downstairs to see the **Great Hall** and then take the cylindrical elevator back up.

When you exit the building, walk up Cooper Square to the black gate behind Starbucks. Although the gate is usually locked, you can peer through the bars at the stone eagle that is one of the 22 stone eagles that guarded the old Pennsylvania Station before it was demolished. The sculptor, Adolph Weinman, is a Cooper Union graduate, and you'll notice that his eagles have heads and legs only, since they were to be viewed from below.

Retrace your steps to Astor Place and walk toward Lafayette Street. The big black cube in the middle of the street is called the *Alamo* and if you give it a hard push it will spin. Continue down Lafayette until you see the Joseph Papp Public Theater on your left, which was formerly the Astor Library. From 1921 to 1965, this building served as the headquarters of the Hebrew Immigrant Aid Society (HIAS), which housed tens of thousands of Jewish refugees escaping religious persecution to start new lives in the states.

Across the street, above the restaurant Indochine, you'll see Colonnade Row, built in 1833. These houses were designed for the city's first millionaires, such as the Astors, the Vanderbilts, and the Thackerays. The solid marble columns, built by Sing Sing prisoners, form a single row to give the impression that each individual resident owned the entire block. You'll notice that the parlor is on the upper floor, or *piana nobile* (noble floor), rather than the bottom floor, with terraces from which the owners could survey the city.

Follow Lafayette down to 4th Street. The building on the northeast corner with the castle-like gates is the DeVinne Press Building, named for the notable nineteenth-century printer Thomas DeVinne. Make a left at the corner and on your left side toward the end of the block you'll stumble onto the **Merchant's House Museum**, which has been meticulously maintained to look like it did in the 1800s, both inside and out.

On Bowery Street walk toward Bond Street, named after the posh area in London, and you will see the Bouwerie Lane Theatre, which used to be the Bond Street Savings Bank. Diagonally across the street is the three-story **Amato Opera Theater**, and two doors down, offering a different kind of music experience, was the famously grungy CBGB & OMFUG or "Country, Blue Grass, Blues and Other Music For Uplifting Gormandizers" the birthplace of punk bands such as Blondie, the Ramones, and the Talking Heads. Like many small landmarks in this neighborhood, the venue was knocked down for luxury residential buildings.

Walk to the corner of Houston and Bowery and turn left to get to the Liz Christy Community Garden, the first community garden in the city, founded in 1973. It is named for the local resident and gardening activist who started a group called the Green Guerillas, members of which sought to beautify the streets botanically. The city rents them the space for $1 a month. The new development next to the garden was the site of McGurk's Suicide Hall. This Civil War–era hotel devolved into a brothel by the 1890s, where six prostitutes simultaneously committed suicide drinking carbolic acid. John H. McGurk capitalized on the exposure brought on by this tragedy by renaming his saloon "McGurk's Suicide Hall."

Continue down Houston and make a left up Second Avenue until you're standing between 2nd and 3rd Streets, where you'll see the New York Marble Cemetery on your left. The New York Marble Cemetery is the city's first nonsectarian burial ground and one of its oldest. From 1830 to 1937, 2,060 New York professionals were buried here, such as James Tallmadge, Jr., the founder of New York University, who is buried in vault 118. The only markings in the graveyard are the marble plaques set into the north and south walls that bear the family names of the deceased. The gate is usually locked, making it difficult to do more than peek at the grounds. A sister New York Marble Cemetery sits around the corner at 2nd Street between First and Second Avenues on the left side of the street, and this gate, spanning almost the entire block, offers a complete view.

At the end of 2nd Street, make a right, walk down a block, and you will find yourself standing on 1st and First. In a *Seinfeld* episode, Kramer winds up here and exclaims, "I'm on 1st and First! How can the same street intersect with itself? I must be at the nexus of the universe!"

TOMPKINS SQUARE PARK

The park was once part of the estate of Daniel D. Tompkins, who was governor of New York from 1807 to 1817 and vice president under James Monroe. Originally created to lure prospective homeowners to the eastern boundary of New York, the park ultimately became a commons for immigrant and working-class residents of the surrounding tenements. Throughout the nineteenth century, various union marches and

labor demonstrations took place here, and the park became a starting point for marches on City Hall. The park also served as a military parade ground throughout the Civil War. By the 1960s, the park was the setting for Vietnam protest demonstrations and a gathering place for political activists, as well as a gritty crime- and drug-ridden area.

The park served as the site of the founding of the Hare Krishna religion on October 9, 1966, commemorated by a sacred elm tree planted in its center, as well as the venue for the first East Coast Grateful Dead concert. Recent protest issues have included gay rights, homelessness, affordable housing, and police brutality, which is particularly appropriate considering that many of the demonstrations here have been marred with violence. In the summer of 1988, for example, the Tompkins Square Riots erupted when police tried to evacuate the park's homeless population. The avant-garde spirit of the East Village continues to this day with the outdoor drag queen festival *Wigstock*, which originated in 1985 as part of the larger *Howl* festival, a literary event inspired by Allen Ginsberg's provocative poem of the same name.

SLOCUM MEMORIAL FOUNTAIN

The fountain, featuring two children looking seaward, stands as a tribute to the 1,000 New Yorkers who died on the triple-decker General Slocum steamship on June 15, 1904. The excursion steamer provided working-class citizens the opportunity to get out of the city with their families and onto the New York waterways. On the day of the accident, the wooden ship took a different course than usual to bring its mostly German immigrant passengers to Locust Grove, Long Island, for a St. Mark's Lutheran church outing. Twenty minutes after its departure, the storage room caught on fire and soon after the entire boat was ablaze. The crew didn't know how to handle emergencies, the life vests were defective, and the

majority of the passengers didn't know how to swim, which resulted in entire families drowning. It was especially tragic that most of the victims were young children. The East Village German community, Kleindeutschland, held funerals every hour in the weeks that followed, and many devastated family members committed suicide. Until September 11, 2001, this tragedy resulted in the highest death toll in New York City history, including the sinking of the *Titanic*. The fountain, which sits in the children's playground, was designed by Bruno Louis Zimm and donated by the Sympathy Society of German Ladies in 1906.

St. Mark's Church in the Bowery

Erected in 1795, this Episcopal Church belonged to Dutch governor Peter Stuyvesant, now buried underneath, who used it as a private chapel. The chapel is the oldest in continuous use by Christian congregations in New York. By the 1960s, the space became a progressive landmark when the Black

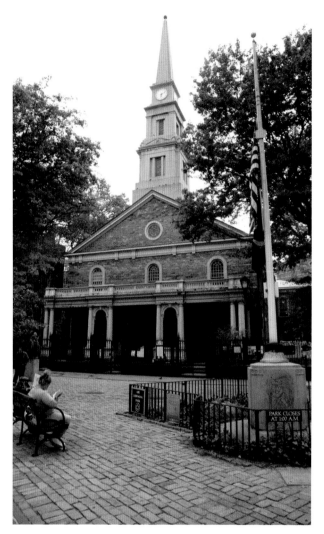

Panthers and Young Lords gathered here. Allen Ginsberg and other prominent writers also started the ongoing St. Mark's Poetry Project in this space. The church was almost completely destroyed by a fire in 1978, but has since been rebuilt, and now serves as an art, dance, music, and cultural event venue. If you glance west from the church you'll see Stuyvesant Street, one of the very few diagonal streets remaining in Manhattan besides Broadway, and the site of an early nineteenth-century farmers' market.

McSorley's

McSorley's is one of New York's oldest bars, dating back to 1854 when John McSorley modeled it after a public house in Ireland. In 1890 he passed the establishment onto his son Bill, who ran the bar until the family sold it in 1936. Although Bill never touched alcohol, he served indiscreetly throughout Prohibition in the safety of his politician regulars. In fact, McSorley's was the only legally operating bar in New York during Prohibition. When the McSorley family ran the bar, they personally opened and closed it every night, and served a complimentary last round of drinks at closing time.

The bar didn't serve women until 1970, when the Supreme Court established the McSorley Law based on this case, which outlaws discrimination in public places. Even with the law, a women's bathroom wasn't added until 1986.

The bar has an authentic Irish pub feel due to its relatively bright lighting, communal tables, and weathered memorabilia lining the walls. This memorabilia includes Harry Houdini's cufflinks and an original want ad for John Wilkes Booth after he assassinated President Lincoln. World War I soldiers hung wishbones on the dusty chandelier for good luck, and the ones that are still hanging represent the men who never returned. The floor is covered in sawdust, the music is barely audible over the bar conversation, and bartenders wear garbage bags under their aprons to guard against spills. Additionally, the taps run light and dark McSorley Ale only—no other beer, wine, or even coffee. When you order one drink, you're given two, which necessitates that everyone "double fist" (if you order a "one and one" they'll give you one of each). There are long lines here on weekend nights, and lines around the corner on St. Patrick's Day. As the "be good or be gone" sign suggests, they often have to throw patrons out for rowdiness. The best time to take in the ambiance is during the day when the bar is at its mellowest.

Cooper Union for the Advancement of Science and Art

Peter Cooper (1791–1883) started out in poverty as the son of a hat maker, and had less than a year of formal schooling over the course of his life. He made his first fortune from glue in the 1820s. One of the byproducts of glue is gelatin, so Peter Cooper also inadvertently invented Jello (his wife was working on flavors and colors when she died). In the 1830s Cooper focused his energies on railroads and created the first steam-powered railroad engine, which he named "Tom Thumb." He later built the largest rolling mill in the country for railroad iron, as well as the first structural wrought iron beams. His character was such that when he realized he was making more money than he should have been, he lowered the prices of iron rails for his customers instead of pocketing the profits for himself.

Cooper dabbled successfully in real estate, railroads, and telegraphy, and even ran for president in 1876. Most impressive, however, was Cooper's conviction that every person deserved an education "as free as the air we breathe and the water we drink," which prompted him to found Cooper Union for the Advancement of Science and Art in 1858. The tuition-free school prepared children of immigrants and the working class for careers in business, and refused to discriminate on the basis of race, religion, or sex. The caliber of students at Cooper Union has always been high due to its extremely low (10–12 percent) acceptance rate, making it one of the most selective schools in the United States, so it's no surprise that Thomas Edison was an alumnus. It has remained a full-scholarship institution ever since its inception, generating tuition money from the ground grant of the farmland property Peter Cooper bought under the Chrysler Building.

In 1859 the Cooper Union was the tallest building in New York City. As the first fireproof structure in the city, it also set a standard for public safety in construction. As part of its then cutting-edge design, Cooper requested a round shaft in anticipation of a pneumatic vacuum elevator, but by the time the building was completed, elevators were mechanical. The shaft stood empty until the 1970s, when a cylindrical elevator was added.

The Great Hall

The 1858 Great Hall in the downstairs area of Cooper Union has served as a lecture space for leaders in various fields, including science, art, and politics. From this podium, the voices of the NAACP, the women's suffrage movement, and the American Red Cross have reached the masses. Several presidential candidates have spoken here, including Lincoln, Grant, Cleveland, Taft, Roosevelt, Wilson, and Clinton. The stage is high because of the peanut gallery, so named for the standing-room only crowd that would buy hot peanuts and spit out the shells on the floor.

In 1860 Abraham Lincoln gave his famous anti-slavery speech in the Great Hall, which he concluded, "Let us have faith that right makes might, and in that faith, let us, to the end, dare to do our duty as we understand it." Today an image of Lincoln hangs on the wall directly across from the podium. Lincoln intended to give this speech in antislavery Brooklyn instead of proslavery New York (two different cities at the time), but February 27, 1860, was a wet and stormy night and Brooklyn didn't have a bridge yet, so he spoke here instead. The speech, combined with a campaign brochure featuring a photograph taken by Matthew Brady, who only included the top half of Lincoln's lanky body, helped catapult Lincoln to victory.

Merchant's House Museum

In 1835 Seabury Treadwell bought this Federal-style house on what was then the outermost part of New York. He lived here with his wife and seven children, the youngest of whom was his daughter Gertrude. She

wanted to marry an Irish Catholic but the devoutly Protestant Seabury forbade her, so she lived in this house for 93 years alone, until her death in 1933. If you look inside, you'll notice that there are no closets in the house because when it was built houses were taxed by number of rooms and closets counted as rooms.

AMATO OPERA THEATER

In 1948 Tony and Sally Amato founded the Amato Opera Theater to make opera universally accessible, and to provide fledgling singers with experience in full-length productions. Many of the original opera performers were World War II veterans. The shows started out free and continue to be cheaper than opera anywhere else in the city. The married team celebrated their fifty-fifth anniversary in the year 2000, the same year 82-year-old Sally died. The duo not only performed in the shows, but also coordinated the costumes, sets, musical direction, staging, and publicity.

The company is known for pulling off grand productions in an intimate setting, even using the small space to its advantage. While the theater's capacity is limited to 107, every seat in the house provides a good view of the stage. Additionally, Tony and Sally's unbounded passion for and dedication to the opera and to each other, have always given the productions a familial feel.

Verdi, Mozart, and Puccini remain Tony Amato's favorite composers, and over the years the Opera House has presented thousands of performances by these and other renowned composers. The company also offers an Operas-in-Brief series, featuring abbreviated versions of full operas with English narration, presented at schools, parks, and community centers.

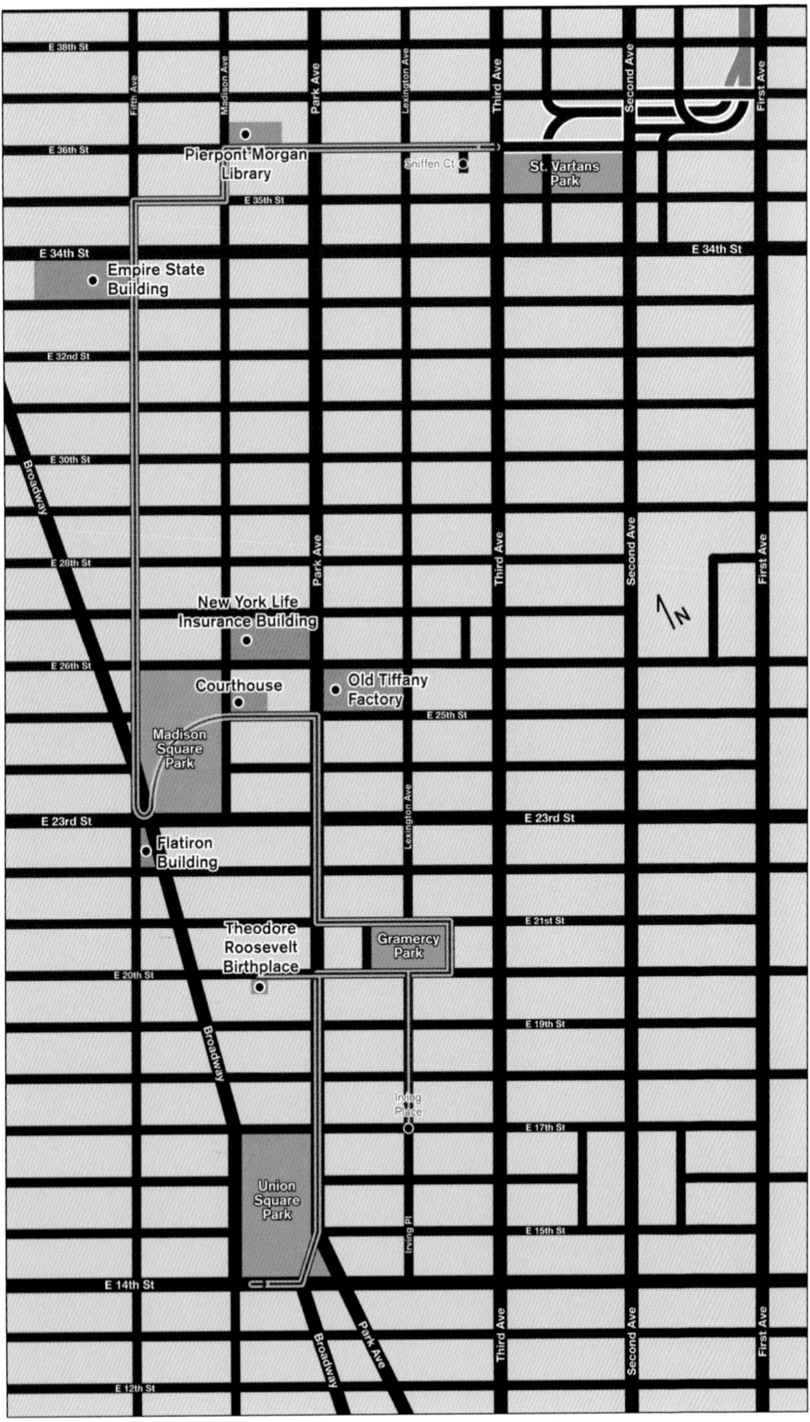
E 38th St
Fifth Ave
Madison Ave
Park Ave
Lexington Ave
Third Ave
Second Ave
First Ave
E 36th St
Pierpont Morgan Library
Sniffen Ct
St. Vartans Park
E 35th St
E 34th St
E 34th St
Empire State Building
E 32nd St
E 30th St
Broadway
E 28th St
Park Ave
Third Ave
Second Ave
First Ave
New York Life Insurance Building
E 26th St
Courthouse
Old Tiffany Factory
E 25th St
Madison Square Park
Lexington Ave
E 23rd St
E 23rd St
Flatiron Building
E 21st St
Theodore Roosevelt Birthplace
Gramercy Park
E 20th St
E 19th St
Broadway
Irving Place
E 17th St
Union Square Park
Irving Pl
E 15th St
E 14th St
Broadway
Park Ave
Third Ave
Second Ave
First Ave
E 12th St

Union Square and Gramercy

Union Square is one of Manhattan's key urban centers. Every subway line connects here, and it is rare for the area to be devoid of demonstrators, skateboarders, and performance artists, or their audiences. Huge chain retailers like Circuit City, Whole Foods, and the Virgin Megastore tower over the park, but the neighborhood has something for everyone. Off-Broadway shows run in local theaters, fresh produce is sold at the outdoor Greenmarket, and some of the city's best restaurants are just a stone's throw away. Additionally, the world's preeminent writers give readings at the 17th Street Barnes & Noble, while Paragon Sports on 19th Street and Broadway offers equipment and gear for every kind of athlete, from snowboarders to kayakers.

Gramercy Park could not feel more different than Union Square, being tucked away in a location that impedes traffic and noise. The small private park is reminiscent of an English garden, and the quaint buildings around the park are just as beautiful as their meticulously landscaped backyard. Because no one can get into the Gramercy Park without a key, it remains one of the quietest places in the city. Madison Square Park nearby is another urban retreat, though not as well hidden, providing just enough greenery to recharge neighborhood office workers.

U nion Square Park was named for the union of Bowerie Lane (now Fourth Avenue) and Bloomingdale Road (now Broadway). To attract potential residents, a fence surrounded the park until 1871. On the south side of Union Square overlooking 14th Street, you'll see a grand statue of George Washington on horseback. Washington is depicted on Evacuation Day, November 25, 1783, when he reclaimed New York from the British. This is the oldest statue in any New York park, sculpted by Henry Kirke Brown and dedicated to the city in 1865. Brown also designed the Abraham Lincoln statue at the north end of the park by 16th Street, which overlooks the outdoor structure known as Ladies Cottage. The open space north of the Ladies Cottage serves as a famous farmers' market, selling fresh produce and baked goods on Monday, Wednesday, Friday, and Saturday year round. In the center of Union Square Park stands an "Independence Flagstaff" with a base that depicts the heroes and villains of the American Revolution.

33 Union Square West, or the Decker Building, sandwiched between Blue Water Grill and Heartland Brewery, is where Andy Warhol moved his silk-screening Factory in 1968. It was on the sixth floor of this building that prostitute-turned-playwright Valerie Solanas shot Warhol three times with silver spray-painted bullets, thinking that he was a vampire. Warhol was pronounced dead at the hospital that night but managed to survive the murder attempt and further injury from the wounds by wearing a corset for the rest of his life. Notice the unusual Moorish style of the upper windows and balconies.

Starting at 15th Street and Union Square East, you'll find a timeline of the history of the park embedded clockwise in the pavement, complete with illustrated bronze plaques. You'll also see the original building of the old Bowery Savings Bank across the street, classically designed with tall columns to inspire virtue and guardianship. The Virgin/Circuit City store on 14th Street is adorned with the 1999 "Metronome," an art project that explores the relationship between the city and time. The black-and-gold rotating sphere signifies the phases of the moon and the digital clock measures the hours of the day backward and forward (from right to left the numbers show how many hours, minutes, and seconds in the day have passed; from left to right, the numbers show how many hours, minutes, and seconds in the day remain). When the Metronome strikes noon, it emits a cloud of steam. The clock is meant to accentuate the southern end of Park Avenue South just as the Grand Central Terminal clock accentuates the northern end.

At the southwest corner of the park, between 14th and 15th Streets, stands a 1986 monument to Indian political reformer Mohandas Gandhi. The memorial celebrates the park's history of nonviolent protest.

Follow Union Square East north until it becomes Park Avenue South. The New York Film Academy School was once the site of **Tammany Hall**. You'll notice that the W Hotel on your right has a "GL" on its third-story terrace because the building used to house the Germania Life Insurance Company before it changed its name to Guardian Life during World War I. Old Town Bar on 18th Street is a German-owned brewery that has been serving drinks and pub food since 1892. Their hamburgers are some of the best in town.

At 20th Street, make a left, and walk to 28 East 20th Street, former President Teddy Roosevelt's birthplace. Although the house itself is not technically the same as the one Roosevelt grew up in, the 1923 replica is almost identical.

Walk back to Park Avenue and over to **Gramercy Park**, New York City's only private park. At Irving Place, turn right and walk down the west side of the street toward 17th Street, passing a cast iron double bishop crook lamp on the corner of 18th Street. Irving Place, which only runs six blocks, is named for writer Washington Irving, who wrote "The Legend of Sleepy Hollow" and "Rip Van Winkle." A tablet marks his 1845 home at the corner of 17th Street, and a bust of his likeness sits across the street on Irving Place. On your way back up to Gramercy Park, notice Sal Anthony's Restaurant, where writer O Henry lived on the second floor from 1902 to 1910, and Pete's Tavern, where O Henry wrote perhaps his best-known story "The Gift of the Magi." On 19th Street between Irving Place and Third Avenue, glance at architect Frederic Sterner's townhouses, which he titled the "Block Beautiful."

Back on Gramercy, walk around the park and exit on 21st Street toward Park Avenue. Cross the street to get a better look at the buildings on the east side of Park Avenue, such as the Lyceum Theater on 312–316 Park Avenue, which was once one of the neighborhood's most famous theaters. Louis Comfort Tiffany and Thomas Edison, both self-taught chemists, met while collaborating on the Lyceum, making it both the first electrically lit theater and the first to employ footlights. Edison also came up with the idea of making lamps incorporating Edison bulbs with Tiffany glass. The Tiffany factory, where the artist perfected the opalescent glass technique seen in his trademark lamps and vases, was located in the red brick buildings on 25th and Park from 1881 to 1905.

25th Street between Park and Lexington is home to the 69th Street Regiment Armory, where the first Armory show took place in 1913. The exhibition allowed unknown modern artists to exhibit work to the general public, and led to the advancement of modern art.

Make a left on 25th Street and walk toward Madison Park. The striking building at the end of the block is the **Courthouse for the Appellate Division, First Department of the New York State Supreme Court**. It is the first of four such courthouses in New York. This division covers New York's original territory of Manhattan and the Bronx and it is one of the busiest appellate courts in the United States.

Walk into the park and turn right. Madison Park represents a fraction of the original area intended for Central Park when Central Park was proposed to be downtown. The site was pared down to this space after plans for Central Park were moved uptown. Rumor has it that this is the park where baseball was conceived in the 1840s, before the game became an official sport. At the north end of the park, you'll see a statue of the 21st president, Chester Alan Arthur, who lived nearby on 28th and Lexington Avenue. Diagonally across the northeast corner of the park is an enormous building with large arches on the ground floor and deep setbacks starting four stories up. This was the original Madison Square Garden that the famous architect Stanford White built and took his last breath in when millionaire Harry K. Thaw shot him in cold blood. At the time, the building was only about as high as the first setback. Now it is the massive New York Life Insurance Building, designed by Woolworth Building architect Cass Gilbert.

Take the path on your left on the northern end of the park, walking toward the center, and you'll see a David Glasgow Farragut Monument on your right. The Italian-style sculpture of this Civil War hero is an early example of the art nouveau movement, characterized by twisting plant forms such as those carved into the glassware of Lalique, and which would come to dictate American art at the start of the twentieth century. On the east side of Madison Square Park across from the entrance to the courthouse are two buildings: one squat, the other tower-shaped with clocks on all sides and a gold crown on top. The gold-topped building is the Met Life Tower, which at 50 stories high in 1909 was the tallest building in the world. The architecture resembles the Campanile di San Marco in Venice because Met Life wanted to publicize their help in restoring the Campanile after it was damaged in a 1902 thunderstorm. The stout Met Life Annex next door looks incomplete because it is incomplete. It was originally designed to be the tallest building in the world, but with the Great Depression Met Life could only afford to build the structure one-third as high as they had intended.

Walk to the southwest corner of the park to the William H. Seward Monument. This former governor of New York lost the Republican nomination to Lincoln in 1860 because he was so radically antislavery that he was considered more likely than Lincoln to instigate a civil war. Nevertheless, he and Lincoln became fast friends and worked together throughout Lincoln's presidency.

Cross Broadway so that you're standing on the second island in the middle of the street. The slim structure dividing Fifth Avenue and Broadway is the

Flatiron Building. Its name comes from the skyscraper's resemblance to a clothing iron. There had never been a freestanding skyscraper before 1902, so even though the Flatiron was never the tallest building in New York City, its height appears inflated. The steel-framed building was designed to withstand powerful wind gusts with a structure that directed wind downward. This resulted in drafts that caused women's skirts to blow up enough to expose their ankles, and men congregating on the street corner to witness this phenomenon.

Continue to Broadway and walk uptown. The obelisk at Worth Square is a tribute to Mexican War–hero General William Worth, who is buried underneath. Turn right on 25th Street and left on Fifth Avenue and walk uptown. On the left side of Fifth Avenue between 33rd and 34th Streets is the **Empire State Building**. If it weren't for the awning you might pass right by it. This is because the tower was built for the skyline and not for the street. The first six stories of the skyscraper were meant to fit in with the other commercial buildings on this block, while the tip was intended to puncture the sky. The building on the right side of the street between 34th and 35th is the CUNY Graduate Center, housed in the former B. Altman Department Store Building, one of the flagship department stores on Fifth Avenue in 1906.

Turn right on 35th Street and walk to Madison Avenue. On the northeast corner of 36th and Madison you'll find the **Pierpont Morgan Library**. As you cross Park Avenue toward the library, glance up the avenue at the Tiffany clock adorning the entrance of Grand Central Terminal. Continue on 36th Street to Lexington Avenue, where you'll see the Soldiers', Sailors', Marines' and Airmen's Club, a hotel founded in 1919 exclusively for members of the US Armed Forces and its allies. Looking north up Lexington Avenue you also have a good view of the Chrysler Building. In the middle of the block between

Lexington and Third Avenues, to your right, is Sniffen Court. Built between 1850 and 1860, this hidden area contains stables that architect John Sniffen converted into townhouses in the 1920s. The far end of the alley, where a hand pump once supplied water to thirsty

horses, displays longtime resident Malvina Hoffman's plaques of Greek horsemen. The Doors' *Strange Days* album cover was shot in this court.

If you walk another block east you will come to St. Vartan Park and playground, to the right of the Queens–Midtown Tunnel. The playground and nearby church are named for the fourth-century Armenian martyr Vartan, and serve the Armenian population in this part of town.

UNION SQUARE PARK

Central Park architects Frederick Law Olmsted and Calvert Vaux designed Union Square Park in 1872; it was demolished in the 1920s for the subway, rebuilt in the 1930s, and renovated in the 1980s. From the time of its inception the park has seen its share of protests and public gatherings. As early as the spring of 1861, 250,000 Union supporters gathered to denounce the southern rebellion after the outbreak of the Civil War. This was the largest crowd assembled in the nation's

history up until that point. In September of 1882, the park marked the conclusion of the city's first Labor Day parade, and labor activist Emma Goldman was arrested here in 1893 for telling the unemployed to steal bread. By the 1960s the park was known as "Needle Park" for its conspicuous drug activity, but the plot was cleaned up in the 1980s and has been functional ever since. After the attacks on the World Trade Center, the park was covered in candles, pictures, and photographs as a tribute to the victims.

Tammany Hall

The northern side of the building reads "The Society of Tammany Hall or Columbian Order" and is dated 1786, which is the year the society was formed. This building was the headquarters of the Democratic Party in Manhattan, known as Tammany Hall. Tammany Hall became highly influential in New York politics starting in the 1840s, when the organization enticed immigrants to join by offering jobs, housing, and even citizenship. In exchange, Tammany Hall required unconditional devotion to the Democratic Party, which translated into voting for the party's candidates, often repeatedly.

The organization lost much of its power in the 1930s after President Franklin Delano Roosevelt investigated its corrupt practices, but reinvented itself as a legitimate institution in the 1950s and continued to serve as an important part of the Democratic Party until the 1960s. A relief bust of the Lenape Indian Chief Tamanand adorns the exterior because an early goal of the organization was to improve the country's image of Native Americans.

Gramercy Park

Gramercy Park first opened in 1844. The land was formerly a swamp, evidenced by its former name, Crommessie, which translates into "crooked swamp" in Dutch. Gramercy is surrounded by private social clubs such as the National Arts Club, founded in 1898 as a gathering place for artists and patrons of the arts. Shakespearean actor Edwin Booth founded the Players Club next door, in order to elevate the status of actors in society. A statue of Booth playing Hamlet stands facing the entrance to Gramercy Park. The park is also bordered by handsome apartment buildings, the residents of which are the sole bearers of the park's keys. Novelist John Steinbeck lived in 13 Gramercy Park North, and classical music composer George

Templeton Strong lived at 60 Gramercy Park North. 3 and 4 Gramercy Park West are reminiscent of traditional southern-style architecture, the likes of which you might find in New Orleans. Former mayor James Harper of the Harper Brothers Publishing Company lived at #4 and had the two "mayoral lampposts" placed in front of his building to distinguish it as the home of the mayor. Every so often the park is open to the public, such as Gramercy Day, the date of which changes annually.

APPELLATE DIVISION, FIRST DEPARTMENT OF THE NEW YORK STATE SUPREME COURT

The socially well-connected James Brown Lord designed this courthouse in 1900 with the help of some of the best American artists of his time. As a Beaux Art structure, a third of the building's budget was allotted to ornamentation appropriate for a house of law. Various American sculptors designed the statues at the top of the building, each figure representing a different school of justice. The figure on the far left is the Hebrew Moses, followed by the Chinese Confucius, Persian Zoroaster, Greek Lycurgus and Solon, Roman Justinian, Anglo-Saxon Alfred the Great, French Louis IX, and the Indian Manu. The empty plinth at the far right held a figure of Islam's Muhammad until it was removed in the 1950s, because Islam forbids any sculpture that might be perceived as iconography of God or religious figures. On either side of the stairs are representations of wisdom and force, two necessary elements of the

law, sculpted by Frederick Wellington Ruckstull. Inside the courthouse, murals by ten different artists depict legal themes. A greater number of sculptors worked on this building than any other in the country.

EMPIRE STATE BUILDING

When the Empire State Building opened on May 1, 1931, it was the tallest building in the world. Built on the site of the old Waldorf-Astoria Hotel, the 102-story building took only a little over a year to build. Its name comes from the nickname for New York State, but due to the building's inability to attract renters, it was known as the "Empty State Building" in its early years. The crown was meant to be a docking station for blimps, which would be anchored to the 102nd floor while serviced, but air drafts and potential explosions posed difficulties. Now the would-be mast is the base of a TV tower, from which almost all of New York's broadcast stations transmit.

In 1931 President Herbert Hoover pressed a button in Washington, DC to turn on the building's distinctive lights. The tower is just as often lit in symbolic colors honoring national holidays, seasons, and cultural events, as it is lit in white. The lights glow red on Valentine's Day, gold during Oscar Week, green on St. Patrick's Day, and orange and blue on New York Knicks Opening Day. The lights are only turned off during certain times of the spring and fall to protect migrating birds from flying toward them, as well as on AIDS Awareness Day and on national days of mourning.

The Empire State Building lost its reputation as the world's tallest building to the World Trade Center in 1972, but continues to be the tallest building until the towers are rebuilt. The colossal skyscraper is a testament to structural achievement and human will, particularly in light of the oppressive Great Depression era in which it was built. There is an 86th-floor observatory and a 102nd-floor observatory, both of which provide expansive views of the city on clear nights.

Pierpont Morgan Library

American financier and banker John Pierpont Morgan, better known as J.P. Morgan, owned this private library, which stood adjacent to his New York mansion. As owner of the first billion-dollar corporation in history and one of the most influential men of his time, J.P. Morgan was so well known that crowds parted to let him pass when he walked down the street. In addition to his financial successes, Morgan was also a philanthropist and one of the preeminent art collectors in the country, as well as the president of the Metropolitan Museum of Art. In fact, at the time of his death, Morgan had the largest private art collection in the world.

Charles McKim of the famous architectural firm McKim, Mead and White built the library between the years 1902 and 1906, and it is considered the architect's masterpiece. Morgan's son Jack dedicated the institution to the city in 1924 in accordance with his father's wishes to share his collection with the public. Today the mansion, library, and a 1928 annex comprise the Morgan Library, which is a museum and scholarly research facility, offering lectures, concerts, and fine art exhibitions. Much of the art here is from J.P. Morgan's personal collection.

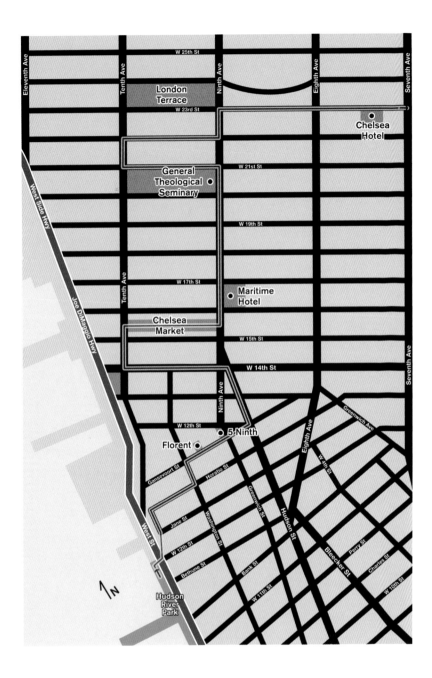

The Meatpacking District and Chelsea

*T*he Meatpacking District and Chelsea were both obscure industrial neighborhoods until the end of the twentieth century. Slaughterhouses and processing plants dominated the area once known as Gansevoort Market in the Meatpacking District, and the patrons at the few food joints in the area were generally the butchers and meatpackers who worked there. In recent years most of the district's meatpackers have moved out, although a handful of distribution plants remain, and upscale bars, retailers, and restaurants are finding creative uses for the trademark cobblestones and warehouse spaces.

Chelsea has gone through a similar gentrification process, and the freight-unloading area once filled with Irish longshoremen that also served as an early center for the motion picture industry, has become the art Mecca of Manhattan. Contemporary art galleries have taken over every available storefront space, and on Thursday evenings when most gallery openings occur, art enthusiasts spill onto the streets and into the local bars and restaurants. There was little to see here back when this area was an industrial hub, but today the waterfront neighborhood that was safely tucked away from the action of the rest of the city is its own hotbed of New York nightlife and culture.

Start:	12th Street and the Hudson River
Finish:	23rd Street and Seventh Avenue
Length:	2 miles
Time:	1.75 hours

Refreshments: Florent for quality comfort food, Paradou for French fare in a garden setting, Markt for mussels, or Pop Burger for quick snacks like mini burgers and milkshakes.
Sights: Hudson River, Florent, Meatpacking District, Wooster Projects, Chelsea Market, Maritime Hotel, General Theological Seminary, London Terrace, the Chelsea Hotel, McBurney YMCA.

Start at the **Hudson River**, entering at West Street and 12th Street, and walk all the way out to the water to take in the view of Hoboken, New Jersey. Once a major transatlantic port, Hoboken has become a reasonably priced alternative to Manhattan living. The 1954 film *On the Waterfront* was shot there, based on the real waterfront corruption in the area at the time.

Exit the park at the ramp, carefully crossing the West Side Highway toward the warehouses of the Meatpacking District. Walk to Horatio Street two blocks up and follow Horatio to Washington Street. At Washington, turn left to get onto Gansevoort Street. **Florent** restaurant is to your right at Gansevoort, offering the fluffiest macaroni 'n' cheese in New York City. Continue down Gansevoort to the large cobblestone plaza of Ninth Avenue. The ivy-covered 1850s townhouse on the corner is 5 Ninth, a creative American restaurant with patio dining in the summer.

Walk up Ninth Avenue, passing the 24-hour French bistro Pastis, where brunch-goers spend entire Sunday afternoons waiting for available tables. The abundance of 24-hour restaurants in the area is due to the loud and late weekend traffic that has come to typify the Meatpacking District. The restaurants are packed and occasionally rowdy, but they are also some of the best late-night food establishments in town. You'll come to an anomaly in the road where Ninth Avenue angles east. This triangular block, fully occupied by the 1886 brick triangle building, is the cornerstone of the neighborhood. The building houses art galleries and a ground floor Italian restaurant by the name of Vento, which has a relatively tame basement lounge compared those of years past, which included a gay leather club called The Manhole and an S&M club called Hellfire. The hotel across the plaza to the east is Hotel Gansevoort, and the pool on its roof has underwater music and lights.

At the apex of the triangular block, look across Greenwich Street at The Gaslight. This low-key bar with wrap-around French doors was a gay sex club by the name of The Toilet in the 1970s. To the left of it is the SoHo House, a members-only club for the bridge and tunnel set. Like Hotel Gansevoort, SoHo House has a rooftop pool, and on summer evenings bar-goers at both pools stare across the way at each other over equally overpriced cocktails.

Among the more conspicuous restaurants in the area is the Belgian Markt across 14th Street, specializing in beer and mussels, and Homestead Steak one block uptown, which has been serving neighborhood-appropriate fare since 1868. The Old Homestead used to be the Tidewater Trading Post, a Hudson River merchant exchange near which Herman Melville worked as a customs inspector.

Turn left on 14th Street and look for Western Beef, a meat locker turned grocery store on the north side of the street. Continue west on 14th Street, browsing the high-end boutiques of the district's most popular shopping street. The Little Pie Company on the north side of the street bakes several varieties of miniature pies, including a surprisingly sweet sugarless mixed-berry pie. A few steps away you'll see the large doors of Jeffrey, known for its extensive designer shoe selection, which is not surprising considering that the store was started by the former shoe buyer of Barney's department store.

At Tenth Avenue, glance to your left at the Liberty Inn, a clandestine hotel on the Gansevoort Peninsula that rents by the hour. The peninsula itself is a remnant of the western edge of Manhattan that was demolished to accommodate ships. Walk up Tenth Avenue, which was Manhattan's original shoreline, to 15th Street. For a cultural detour, the contemporary art gallery Wooster Projects is at 418 West 15th Street, down the block back toward Ninth Avenue.

Staying on Tenth Avenue, cross 15th Street and look for an unmarked set of doors on your right in the middle of the block. This is **Chelsea Market**. Walk through the doors and into the market, where you'll see

florists, bakeries, and wine stores, as well as an indoor waterfall and art by local artists displayed on the walls. Sneak into Fat Witch Bakery on your right for a free sample of their brownies. The whole building used to smell like this bakery back when it was the headquarters of Nabisco at the turn of the century. This is the factory where the Oreo cookie was conceived, before it went on to become the best-selling cookie in the United States. Today the building is home to the Food Network, Oxygen Media, Major League Baseball, and New York's local cable news channel NY1.

As you exit onto Ninth Avenue, notice the Port of New York Authority Inland Terminal, built in 1932 to sort truck shipments. In its time, the building encompassed more square feet of space than any other building in the world, surpassed only by the Pentagon in 1942. Glance back at the strange street division on 14th Street, where Hudson and Greenwich streets merge to form Ninth Avenue, and then continue up Ninth Avenue, where you'll see the Maritime Hotel with its round windows. This building served the National Maritime Union until it was converted into a hotel in 2003. The nightly rates at the Maritime Hotel are equivalent to the monthly rent of the red-and-white brick low-income housing projects across Ninth Avenue. Stroll up Ninth Avenue, which exemplifies Chelsea with its cafés, pet-care stores, and houseware shops, and stop at 20th Street, where you'll come to the **General Theological Seminary**, the oldest seminary of the Episcopal Church. If you glance west, you'll also see the Greek revival townhouses of Cushman Row, built by dry-goods merchant Don Alonzo Cushman in 1840.

Continue to the corner of 21st Street and Ninth Avenue, where you'll find an 1832 Federal-style house in which real estate developer James N. Wells lived and worked. He was one of the major builders responsible for bringing residents into Chelsea in the 1830s. Many of the townhouses on 21st Street have retained their nineteenth-century character. Walk past these houses toward Tenth Avenue, where you'll come to the Catholic Church of the Guardian Angel, founded in 1888, originally popular with sailors and seamen. Continue north to 22nd Street and look for the 1940s art deco Empire Diner up the next block, with a stylized Empire State Building on its roof. Turn right on 22nd Street and take in Chelsea's historic row houses. Note the plaque at 420 West 23rd Street honoring Clement Clarke Moore's 1779 birthplace. Next door, the Frederic Fleming House provides a residence for former homeless people getting back on their feet.

At Ninth Avenue, make a left and stop at the corner of 23rd Street. The massive brick buildings that take up the entire block between 23rd and 24th Streets are London Terrace. The 1930s structure, conceived by real-estate mogul Henry Mandel, was built on Captain Thomas Clarke's old farmland, which the captain had intended to be a retirement home. Its amenities included a sun deck, the largest indoor swimming pool in New York, a garage, and a large private garden in the center, all of which are still here, as well as doormen dressed as London "bobbies," as a play on the name. At the time of its construction, it was one of the largest and most impressive buildings in the world, but due to the Great Depression, Mandel had to foreclose the building in 1934 and ended his life by jumping off of the roof.

Continue on 23rd Street, crossing Ninth Avenue, and look for the Chelsea West Cinema to your right. This theater was the original site of the Roundabout Theatre Company from 1974 to 1984, dedicated to reviving classic plays and musicals. Until 1917, the building on the northwest corner of 23rd and Eighth Avenue was the Grand Opera House, one of many at a time when Chelsea was the center of American theater. The Clearview Chelsea Cinema on the next block looks harmless enough from the outside, but it has been a hangout for corrupt politicians, a gay nightclub called

Galaxy 21, and the Squat Theatre, a Hungarian experimental theater company that was banned from Budapest for their subversive performances. The American Communist Party Headquarters are located across the street at #235. You'll soon come to the **Chelsea Hotel** on your right, which is covered in historical plaques and dedications. Across the street on the northwest corner, the two-toned building with the American flag at its entrance is the **McBurney YMCA**. This original New York Y inspired the Village People's jaunty song by the same name.

Hudson River

The Hudson River is named for British explorer Henry Hudson, who was hired by a Dutch trading company to find the fabled "Northwest Passage" to China in 1609. Instead of finding China, he stumbled onto the New York Harbor, home of the Algonquin, Mohican, and Iroquois civilizations. The Dutch arrivals turned the natural woodlands into a Dutch East India Company trading post, the revenues of which quickly developed the city into a prosperous industrial hub. Throughout the nineteenth and twentieth centuries, the Hudson River served both as

the tail end of an immigrant's journey to America and the start off point for a soldier's expedition to war.

From 1825 to 1870, the Hudson River School represented an approach to painting focused on the rich color and detail of the country's landscapes and wildlife. This was the first artistic period unique to America, when artists were just starting to discover and indulge in the beauty of their country, largely personified by the Hudson River itself. Today the Hudson River is mainly used recreationally, and on a sunny day there are always a number of boats making their way leisurely across the water.

FLORENT

If Florent the restaurant is the soul of the meatpacking district, then Florent the owner is the soul of the restaurant. The "unofficial mayor of the meat market," Florent Morellet opened this 24-hour French bistro in 1986, eight years after moving to the United States. He has successfully campaigned to preserve the neighborhood as a historic district ever since. A crusader not only on behalf of architecture, but also social issues, Florent has mobilized AIDS awareness, pro-choice and right-to-die events, and serves as the president of Compassion in Dying New York. His ever-changing "specials" board displays activist messages, as well as weather reports, flippant observations such as what not to name a baby this year, and a running record of his own T-cell count.

The atmosphere of the restaurant is liveliest late-night, and decadent on the "high holidays": Bastille Day, Halloween, and New Year's Eve, when Florent and his friends celebrate in drag. The R&L restaurant that existed before Florent took over was a traditional American diner, as is evident by the Formica and stainless steel décor and bar stools. If you stick around for the mac 'n' cheese, look for the "specials" board above the bar, and the maps of imaginary cities, drawn by Florent, along the back wall.

GENERAL THEOLOGICAL SEMINARY

Retired British Army officer Captain Thomas Clarke bought the farmland between 19th and 24th Streets west of Eighth Avenue in 1750. He named the neighborhood "Chelsea" after London's Royal Chelsea Hospital for Old Soldiers. Two generations later, Captain Clarke's grandson, Clement Clarke Moore, converted large sections of his inherited property into a suburban neighborhood, and donated the land used for the General Theological Seminary. Founded in 1817, it is the oldest Episcopal Seminary in the United States and houses the St. Mark's Library, with the largest collection of Latin bibles in the country. Perhaps known best for his "'Twas the Night Before Christmas" poem, Clement Clark Moore taught Oriental and Greek literature at the seminary from 1821 to 1850.

The High Line

The High Line was an out-of-use elevated rail constructed between 1929 and 1934 to transport fruit, produce, and meat from boats to the factories around the waterfront without the encumbrance of street traffic. The tracks are suspended between avenues because the street-level tracks that preceded the High Line caused so many accidents that Tenth Avenue came to be known as "Death Avenue." Originally a thirteen-block elevated rail, the railroad was partially dismantled in the 1960s and then abandoned to grassy overgrowth until 2004, when a design team was selected to convert the remaining 1.45 miles of the High Line into a public promenade. When the project is complete, pedestrians will have an elevated park extending from the Meatpacking District to Pennsylvania Station from which to observe the neighborhood while enjoying the serenity of a green space 20 to 30 feet above ground. Until that time, the High Line is considered private property owned by CSX railroad, so adventurous sightseers should be wary not to get caught trespassing.

The Chelsea Hotel

The Chelsea Hotel was New York's tallest building from its construction in 1884 until 1902. Initially intended to be a cooperative apartment house, the building became a hotel in 1905 after the coop went bankrupt. The thick walls insulated practicing musicians inside their rooms, while providing solitude to writers and artists from the outside world. Playwright Arthur Miller wrote *After the Fall*, *Incident at Vichy*, and *The Price* here and Arthur C. Clarke wrote *2001: A Space Odyssey*. Poets Dylan Thomas and James Schuyler and writers Brendan Behan and Thomas Wolfe spent the last years of their lives here. Mark Twain, William Burroughs, and O Henry all stayed here, O Henry under a different name every night, and in 1978 Sid Vicious of the Sex Pistols murdered his girlfriend Nancy in the now-defunct room 100.

Half of the units are rented on long-term leases, and the other half are no-frills hotel rooms, without even basic amenities like room service, ice machines, and cable television. Most rooms do have high ceilings and fireplaces, however, and a wrought-iron staircase runs from the lobby to the twelfth floor. The lobby also carries several art guides to local galleries, and artwork from past and current building residents hangs on the walls.

McBurney YMCA

The McBurney YMCA is the oldest branch of the Young Man's Christian Association. Irish immigrant Robert Ross McBurney started the organization in 1869, at which time Chelsea was the center of the shipping industry, and this "Seamen's YMCA" provided low-cost housing for nautical workers. Although the YMCA became an interdenominational community center, it started off as an evangelist organization, with Sunday schools, Bible classes, and missionary efforts, like its London and Boston counterparts. Artists Andy Warhol and Keith Haring stayed here, as well as playwright Edward Albee, and Merrill and Lynch met in the swimming pool in 1913. Among the benefits of membership are childcare, sports, arts, and educational programs.

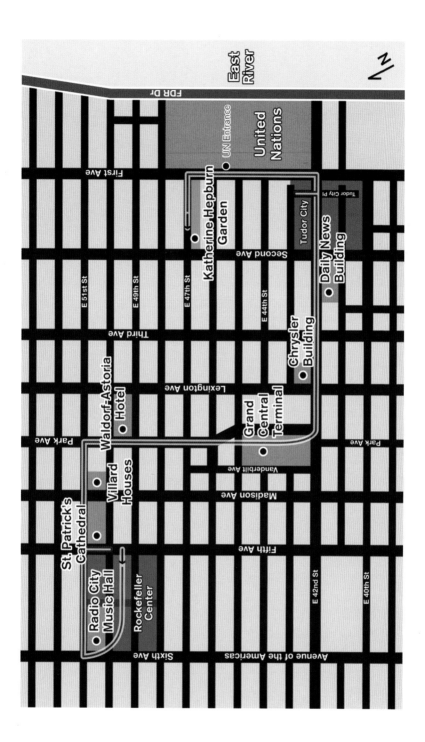

Midtown East

idtown Manhattan is the most economically dense area of the world, partly because of the simplicity of the street grid, but largely because of its use of vertical space. After World War I, the United States' industrial resources had remained intact, which gave the country an advantage over other technologically advanced cities that had to rebuild.

Most of the art deco buildings in Manhattan were built between 1923 and 1932, after which time the production of skyscrapers halted because of the Great Depression. The fiercely geometric and stylized floral-patterned architecture found its roots in 1920s French decorative arts, German expressionism, and New York zoning laws, which required skyscrapers to allow light to pass through a building in proportion to its height. Architects thrived on the challenge of these zoning laws, such as the requirement that the top of the building take up no more than 25 percent of the mass of its base, and they tried to create visually dramatic towers that manipulated the eye upward. They also sought to emphasize a building's three-dimensionality, which is why there is rarely flat ornamentation on or inside these buildings. The ascendant style of art deco architecture embodies New York City's transformation in the Roaring Twenties into the world's modern metropolis.

The Midtown East Walk

Start:	Fifth Avenue between 49th and 50th Streets
Finish:	47th Street between First and Second Avenues
Length:	1.75 miles
Time:	1.75 hours

Refreshments: Haru for sushi, Cipriani 42nd Street for upscale Italian, Comfort Diner for diner food, Mama Mexico for fresh guacamole and festive décor.

Sights: Rockefeller Center, GE Building, Radio City Music Hall, St. Patrick's Cathedral, Villard Houses, Waldorf-Astoria Hotel, Grand Central Terminal, Chanin Building, Chrysler Building, Ford Foundation Building, Tudor City, United Nations.

The open area between 49th and 50th Streets on Fifth Avenue is the **Rockefeller Center** Promenade. Millionaire John D. Rockefeller, Jr. bequeathed these four identical buildings on Fifth Avenue to European countries for the sake of diplomacy. The two buildings on the right between 50th and 51st Streets are actually wings of the taller International Building behind it. The house on the far left is La Maison Francaise, followed by the British Empire Building, then the Palazzo D'Italia and Deutsches Haus, designated for Italy and Germany, respectively. With the onset of World War II, Germany's house was renamed "International Building North" and continues to go by this name. Each country decorated its own entrance. As you can see by the façade, the French chose to emphasize revolution, international relations, and the arts, with images of ancient and modern France, female figures symbolizing poetry, beauty, and elegance, and the inscription "Liberté, égalité, fraternité," the motto of the French Republic. The British entrance projects economic and political dominance; the royal crest and nine high-relief figures represent the nation's thriving industries, whereas the Italians decided on a simple and elegant organic design. Between the two buildings on the right stands the Atlas sculpture designed by Lee Lawrie, who was responsible for most of the art in Rockefeller Center. Atlas's exaggerated musculature and stylized physique are characteristic of the art deco style. The sculpture was picketed upon its unveiling because Atlas was thought to have Mussolini's face. The gardens that sit between the English and French buildings are known as the "Channel Gardens."

As you walk through the gardens to the main part of the center, you might notice that the floor is slanted to hasten your pace. This is a deliberate architectural effort to lure pedestrians into the shops and restaurants. The main statuary in the plaza is the eighteen-foot-high Prometheus, brother to Atlas in Greek mythology. Behind this statue looms the 70-story GE Building, once the RCA Building, and now known as "30 Rock," the home of NBC Studios. The Top of the Rock observation deck on the top floor offers a nice view of Central Park and northern Manhattan. All of Rockefeller Center falls into one zoning lot, providing enough open space on the ground for a tower of this magnitude in the sky.

Walk into the lobby of the GE Building and notice the murals covering the walls and ceilings. Picasso and Matisse were initially approached to craft these frescos, but upon their reluctance to work on such a bourgeoisie project Diego Rivera was called in. Rivera magnificently portrayed a proletariat uprising with Lenin as the leader, but the communist theme didn't go over well with Rockefeller, so his artwork was replaced with that of Spanish artist Jose Maria Sert, who painted industrious workmen raising the city.

Walk all the way to the other side of the GE Building so that you exit at Avenue of the Americas.

You'll be surrounded by huge glass skyscrapers characteristic of this corporate part of town. On your right is **Radio City Music Hall**. Turn right on 50th Street and walk to Fifth Avenue and, if it's open, wander into **St. Patrick's Cathedral**. Saks Fifth Avenue, opened by Adam Gimbel in 1924, is next door. Saks was the first department store to concern itself with the artistic presentation of its windows, and they display seasonal clothing in elaborate settings year round.

Follow 50th Street to the large brown palace on Madison Avenue. Henry Villard, the owner of the Northern Pacific Railroad, had these Villard Houses built in 1884. The hotel that sits above them is the Palace Hotel (formerly the Helmsley Palace). Today the north wing houses the Municipal Arts Society, an organization that advocates public art and historic preservation.

Continue to Park Avenue, where you'll hear the rumbling of the Long Island Rail Road underneath your feet. Be especially careful crossing this street because there are no "Walk" signs on this block. This is because the area beneath you is completely hollow but for railroad tracks. The church across Park Avenue is St. Bartholomew's Church, designed by preeminent architect Stanford White.

Across 50th Street is the **Waldorf-Astoria Hotel**. What you can't see from here is an old subway station that still exists beneath the hotel, built in the 1930s solely for the transportation needs of President Franklin Delano Roosevelt. Confined to a wheelchair by polio, FDR rode in a 1936 Ford convertible equipped with hand controls that made it possible for him to drive. The automobile fit directly onto a train car that stopped at an elevator underneath the Waldorf, enabling Roosevelt to move from his car to his wheelchair out of view of the American public.

Before you enter the Waldorf, take a moment to look at the GE building again, now to your west. The architecture includes a variety of art deco elements, such as vertical window lines, the use of color, setbacks, abstract geometric patterning, and curved corners. Originally the home of RCA, the crown was designed to suggest radio waves. The spire intentionally contains the same colors and materials as the church next door so as to blend in with its neighbor, and the color of the rear wall fades to provide the church with a scenic backdrop.

You'll find that the **Waldorf-Astoria** itself takes up an entire city block. The exterior generally fits in with the other art deco buildings in the area, yet it includes Victorian touches, such as the human figures carved into the sides. Even the entrance features geometric patterns above the doorway and female figures on either side, showing architecture at odds with itself. Walk into the Waldorf and make your way to the main public room where concierge and reception are located. The clock in the center is a relic from the hotel's previous incarnation. Note that the columns in this room are clearly deco, but the room itself is classically decorated with female figures, baskets of flowers, and rich colors.

As you leave the Waldorf, walk down Park Avenue, and you'll find that all of the office buildings, many of which are occupied by international banks and major corporations, forfeit the use of their ground floors. This is due to the noise and vibration of the train running under Park Avenue. The Helmsley Building, built by the New York Central Railroad along with Grand Central Terminal, stands at what appears to be the end of Park Avenue. Walk through East Helmsley Walk and through the MetLife Building, which used to be the Pan Am Building with a heliport on the roof, and continue down the escalator and into **Grand Central Terminal**. Although most refer to it as "Grand Central Station" because it is easier to say, it is more accurately "Grand Central Terminal" because the building traditionally marked the end of a journey to New York rather than a stop along the way.

The stately terminal was designed to evoke an overwhelming impression for new arrivals. If you make your way down to the Oyster Bar Restaurant, you'll discover the Whispering Gallery. Because of the acoustic quality of the tiled archways, sound carries from diagonal to diagonal, so if you are standing beneath one archway and someone else is standing beneath a diagonal archway, you can whisper to each other and the bell dome will carry your voice. Exit the terminal through the doors directly across from the escalator from which you entered. You'll walk through Vanderbilt Hall, which served as a formal waiting room for trains with men and women's lounges at either side. An identical space above it was once a ballroom but is now tennis courts for the CBS Building. As you come to the outer doors, you'll notice that you're walking uphill. Like Rockefeller Center, the effect is to draw people into the terminal.

Make a right at the bridge with a seashell motif as a nod to Vanderbilt's Staten Island ferry, and cross 42nd Street to get to the Lincoln Building. Inside is not a replica of the Lincoln Monument in Washington, DC, but rather Daniel Chester French's original small-scale sculpture upon which the monument is based. Note Lincoln's off-kilter bowtie, signifying that he is truly a man of the people, and his eyes staring down the road into the nation's future. As you exit the Lincoln Building, you'll see an eagle perched on the corner of Grand Central Terminal leftover from the building that was demolished to make way for this one. The Tiffany Clock at the top of the terminal is adorned by Mercury, god of speed and commerce, riding a trademark American eagle, and on the right is graced by Minerva, goddess of intellect and wisdom, and on the left by Hercules, god of strength and power. The Tiffany Clock is bigger than it seems; each Roman numeral is taller than you are.

Walk back down 42nd Street, past the Whitney gallery in the lobby of the Phillip Morris Building, and past Cipriani restaurant, housed in the old Bowery Savings Bank. The building closest to you on the downtown corner of Lexington Avenue is the Chanin Building. Built for the wealthy developer Irwin Chanin in 1929, the building was erected in 205 days. The exterior has several levels of intricate ornamentation, including a level that illustrates the evolutionary development of single-celled creatures to fish and birds, a level that features sea serpents, and a level embellished with stylized flowers. The lobby's themes are "City of Opportunity" and "The Active Life of the Individual," both of which illustrate the American dream that Chanin's life exemplified. Diagonally across the street are the sunburst tower and luminous gargoyles of the **Chrysler Building**.

Continue east on 42nd Street past Third Avenue, and you'll come to the News Building on your right. Architect Raymond Hood designed this whimsical building for the *Daily News* in 1930. The newspaper has since moved to the West Side, but the lobby still holds the world's largest interior globe. The large brown greenhouse building on the left side of 42nd Street is the Ford Foundation Building. Designed to provide a pleasant work atmosphere, its vegetation changes with the seasons and the gardens are open to the public on weekdays.

Ascend the stairs behind the Ford Foundation Building to get to Tudor City. This twelve-building apartment and hotel complex was named for England's Tudor Dynasty (1485–1603), which propelled England out of the Middle Ages and into a major world power. Real estate tycoon Fred F. French built the neighborhood between 1925 and 1928 as a middle-class urban development project. The buildings face inward because the area originally consisted of tenements and slaughterhouses. From Tudor City Place you can look out onto the **United Nations Headquarters**, the East River, and Queens. The cliff overlooking the river was known as Corcoran's Roost in the 1880s, because of the rowdy Corcoran's Roosters gang that occupied a brownstone here. The Tudor City greens near the south side of the complex are often open to the public and make a nice resting spot.

Exit Tudor City at its north side, by the Secretariat Building, along the staircase inscribed with a pacifistic quote: "They shall beat their swords into plowshares, and their spears into pruning hooks. Nation shall not lift up sword against nation, neither shall they learn war any more" (Isaiah 2:4). Ralph Bunche Park at the bottom of the steps was named for the late Nobel Prize–winning UN mediator, and his artist friend, Daniel Larue Johnson, erected the stainless-steel sculpture called *Peace Form One*. The official entrance to the UN is on 46th Street. If you make a left on 47th Street, you'll come across the Katherine Hepburn Garden, which often features public art displays and public speakers.

ROCKEFELLER CENTER

Rockefeller Center is midtown Manhattan's public square. It originally served as a botanical garden for Columbia University's campus, but John D. Rockefeller, Jr. leased the land as a new opera house for the Metropolitan Opera, which at the time was on 39th Street and Broadway. His goal was to have a complex of buildings, the rents from which would subsidize the opera house. With the stock market crash of 1929, the Metropolitan Opera decided to stay in their 39th Street theater, so Rockefeller built Radio City Music Hall instead. Nobody in the city was building at the time because of the Great Depression, so Rockefeller seized the opportunity to use cheap labor and materials for his fourteen-building development, and provided jobs for a quarter million workers during the Depression.

The rectangular sunken plaza in the middle of the center was originally designed for the opera company, and was too low and dark to serve any other obvious

purpose. Someone in the Rockefeller organization suggested using it as an ice-skating ring temporarily, and the ring, surrounded by flags of all nations, has been a New York institution ever since. Construction workers put up the first Christmas tree during the Christmas season of 1931 and a Christmas tree overlooking the plaza soon became a holiday tradition. In recent years the trees have reached heights of 100 feet, with electric lights exceeding 25,000 bulbs, all of which glow with the press of a button at the annual tree lighting in December. After Christmas, the largest part of the trunk is donated to the US Equestrian Team and used as an obstacle jump in their training course. The ring turns into an outdoor café in the summer.

Radio City Music Hall

Radio City Music Hall opened in 1932 through the combined effort of John D. Rockefeller, Jr., the Radio Corporation of America, who later leased the RCA Building in Rockefeller Center for their offices, and "Roxy" Rothafel, who was famous for reviving struggling theaters with Vaudeville movies and décor. Together they built the biggest indoor theater in the world with a stage as technically close to flawless as any of its kind, and a custom-designed "Mighty Wurlitzer" organ that is housed in eleven rooms. Constructed as a variety playhouse, the theater instead chose to show first-run films with stage shows. Among the movies that have opened here are *King Kong*, *Breakfast at Tiffany's*, and *To Kill A Mockingbird*, which established former Radio City usher Gregory Peck as a star. The theater is best known today for its Christmas Spectacular starring the Radio City Rockettes, a holiday tradition since 1932.

St. Patrick's Cathedral

Over 3 million people visit the largest gothic Catholic cathedral in the United States annually. The design alone is reason to visit, with upward-reaching spires 330 feet high, a Latin cross-shaped foundation, and altars designed by Tiffany and Company and Paolo Medici of Rome. New York's archbishops are buried in a crypt beneath the high altar, while their hats hang from the ceiling over their tombs. St. Patrick's was originally meant to be a Catholic cemetery, but its impenetrable foundation of solid rock lent itself more readily to a massive cathedral. Its prime location is due partly to the large Irish population living in the city at the time of its construction.

The Waldorf-Astoria

The reason for the building's unusual combination of art deco and Victorian design is that this isn't the first Waldorf-Astoria. The original structure consisted of two mansions built back-to-back by Astor brothers on the current site of the Empire State Building. One brother named his mansion "Waldorf" after the Astor's farm in Walldorf, Germany, and the other "Astoria" for the Astor family. In the 1890s both families moved to London and decided to merge their manors into one large hotel. At the time the only ballrooms in the city were in private homes, but the Waldorf-Astoria's could hold 400, originating the term "the New York 400." By the 1920s, Prohibition put a damper on the parties at the Waldorf-Astoria and the hotel was sold, relocating to 50th and Park Avenue in 1931, where it has been ever since. Structurally the new building was designed like the other skyscrapers in the area, but internally the décor is Victorian because the owners didn't want to scare off their regular customers.

GRAND CENTRAL TERMINAL

Grand Central Terminal was constructed between 1903 and 1913 by two teams of architects, Reed and Stem, who did the engineering, and Warren and Wetmore, who did the ornamental detailing. The indoor plaza was created to produce a sensation of being outside with a twelve-story-high sky ceiling, which displays one of the biggest murals in the world. The constellations are said to be intentionally upside down because this is God's view of the stars from heaven. The terminal is designed for function as well as form, as is evident by the exits flooded with natural light, where travelers can see where they're going, the wide ramps for luggage, and the palatial staircases that offer a surveying point of the room.

The most beautiful structure in New York City owes its existence to the now least beautiful structure: Pennsylvania Station. Currently functioning out of the basement of Madison Square Garden, Penn Station was

once a magnificent architectural jewel above ground. It was demolished for the sports arena in 1963 before the city established landmark laws. Grand Central Terminal was set for the same fate in 1968, but former First Lady Jacqueline Kennedy rushed to Washington, DC on a train ride referred to as the "Landmark Express" to save the glorious building. The case went as far as the Supreme Court before landmark preservation laws were established. Grand Central Terminal became a landmark in 1967 and a plaque commemorating Jackie Kennedy hangs in Vanderbilt Hall.

THE CHRYSLER BUILDING

The Chrysler Building was constructed as a monument to automobile mogul Walter P. Chrysler, as is evident by the car detailing on its exterior, and was meant to be the tallest building in the world. During the race to the

heavens in the 1920s, the Chrysler architect went head to head with the Bank of the Manhattan Company architect, who was threatening to build the tallest building in the world in the financial district. Both men built the highest skyscrapers possible, but just when it looked like the Bank of the Manhattan Company was going to win with its lantern and flagpole additions, a

185-foot steel spire that had been built inside the Chrysler Building's fire shaft was revealed. The Chrysler architect won, but within a year the Empire State Building overshadowed his masterpiece.

United Nations Headquarters

The term "United Nations" in its earliest usage referred to the 26 nations fighting together in World War II against the Axis Powers. Roosevelt coined the term for an organization that would settle international matters peacefully and codify rules of warfare, similar to the League of Nations after World War I. 50 countries ratified the UN charter in 1945, and currently the organization has 191 member countries. The UN holds 5,000 meetings per year, covering topics ranging from human rights to endangered species to international peace.

John D. Rockefeller, Jr. donated the land for the UN, which extends to the East River. The buildings, not surprisingly, were designed by committee. The wide 39-story green glass building is the Secretariat, to the left is the General Assembly, and directly behind it is the Conference Building. The dome on the General Assembly, an American touch, symbolizes a new world capital. Completed in 1953, the complex is not a part of New York or even the United States, but rather an international zone with its own stamps and post office.

Among the points of interest on the 18-acre site are the various sculptures promoting peace, such as the 256-pound Shinto Peace Bell. After a 1952 session in which 60 UN officials brainstormed a universal symbol of peace, they came up with this imaginative bell gong cast in Japan of tinkling coins from over 60 countries. The bell is inscribed "Long Live Absolute World Peace," and rings every September to open the General Assembly.

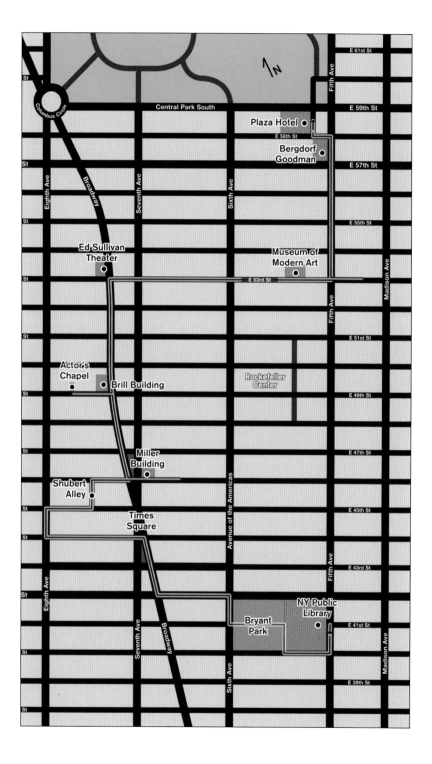

Midtown West

*L*ike Las Vegas in the desert, Times Square presents an extreme contrast to the comparatively neutral landscape of the rest of the city. The area is filled with so much light and life that the middle of the night more often resembles the middle of the day. The neighborhood became the theater district in the Roaring Twenties, and was also known as the "Great White Way," due to the abundance of glittering signs made of white neon lights. The largest of these signs were called spectaculars and they were so bright that they actually stopped traffic. After the Great Depression, the neighborhood deteriorated until the 1990s, when the Disney store opened, prompting other family-friendly businesses to follow suit.

Today, like Vegas, Times Square mostly caters to tourists and families, with a large amount of restaurants, hotels, and attractions. The most famous of these attractions is undoubtedly the Broadway shows, which generate billions of dollars annually. The 39 large-scale theaters that comprise "Broadway" are required to have at least 500 seats and have featured the longest-running plays and musicals in the world, the most enduring of which remains *The Phantom of the Opera*. As the most visually stimulating neighborhood in New York, the spectacle outside of the theaters no doubt rivals the entertainment within.

The Midtown West Walk

Start:	The New York Public Library, 42nd Street and Fifth Avenue
Finish:	The Plaza Hotel, 59th Street and Central Park South
Length:	1.75 miles
Time:	2 hours

Refreshments: Carmine's for groups, Ruby Foo's for family-friendly Pan-Asian, Carnegie Deli for overpriced New York deli food, Brasserie 8 1/2 for French fare and minimalist chic ambiance.

Sights: The New York Public Library, Bryant Park, American Standard Building, Times Square, One Times Square, Sardi's, Shubert Alley, Miller Building, the "Actor's Chapel," "Tin Pan Alley," the Museum of Modern Art (MoMA), Tiffany's, Bergdorf Goodman, the Plaza Hotel.

Note: For discounted tickets to Broadway shows, try the TKTS booth at Broadway and 47th Street on the day of the performance. The booth offers reductions of 25–50 percent on full-price tickets between 3PM and 8PM for evening performances, between 10AM and 2PM for Wednesday and Saturday matinees, and between 11AM and 3PM for Sunday matinees. Be forewarned that the lines are very long and your first-choice show may not be available. There is an additional TKTS booth at South Street Seaport. Go to www.tdf.org/tkts for more information. Special student rates are also available for same-day tickets at theaters with valid ID.

The **New York Public Library** is the grand building on Fifth Avenue, spanning 40th to 42nd Streets. Perhaps its most notable feature is the lions on either side, at first named Leo Astor and Leo Lenox after founders John Jacob Astor and James Lenox, and later renamed Patience and Fortitude in the 1930s by Mayor Fiorello LaGuardia, who encouraged New Yorkers to take on these attributes to get through the Great Depression.

At 40th Street, turn right, and walk toward **Bryant Park** directly behind the library. The black-and-gold building to your left is the Bryant Park Hotel, formerly the American Standard Building. This building, constructed in 1924 by famous art deco architect Raymond M. Hood, is one of the first examples of a skyscraper with a boldly colorful exterior. The building was meant to resemble a fiery radiator like those manufactured by the American Standard heating and air-conditioning company. Stroll through Bryant Park and exit on 41st Street so that you're facing the tall building with the white vertical stripes. Known as the New York Telephone Building, the 1974 skyscraper now houses Verizon. Its marble stripes echo the posterior of the New York Public Library. The sloping Grace Building on the north side of the park is a creative approach to zoning laws that require tall buildings to take up less space as they rise.

Turn left on 42nd Street and walk west. It's impossible to miss the dazzling lights of **Times Square**. As early as World War I, 42nd Street was the heart of the theater district, so much so that theaters on 41st and 43rd Streets had hallways extending to 42nd Street for the street address. Walk up Seventh Avenue and stop at the metal grating that reads "U.S. Armed Forces Recruiting Station." This small military recruiting booth, adorned by neon-lit American flags on either side, enlists more Americans into the military than any other recruiting station in the country. It is not surprising that in the 1960s this station was a popular gathering spot for anti-Vietnam protests. Turn around and look across the street to **One Times Square** with the famous steaming Cup O'Noodles ad on top. New Year's Eve revelers pack into these streets, shoulder to shoulder, to watch the ball drop. MTV's Total Request Live Studio (TRL), occasionally recognizable by the younger viewers loitering outside, is on the corner of 44th Street.

Make a left here and you'll come to the Sam S. Shubert Theatre on your right, named for the middle Shubert brother, a partner in the most powerful theatrical management and production team in the twentieth century. Behind the Shubert sits the Broadhurst, named for playwright George Broadhurst, followed by the Majestic, where *The Phantom of the Opera* has been playing since 1988. Across the street you'll see **Sardi's** restaurant, and behind it the Helen Hayes Theatre, named for the famous Broadway actress, and the St. James Theater, named for the homonymous theater in London. The Rodgers and Hammerstein musical *Oklahoma!* premiered at the St. James in 1943, revolutionizing the industry with its integration of dance, music, and drama into one cohesive show.

At Eighth Avenue, walk with the traffic to 45th Street and turn right, making your way past the Golden, Schoenfeld, and Booth Theaters on your right and the Imperial and Music Box Theaters on your left. The Music Box Theater was one of the few to remain operational during the Depression, due to its production of the Pulitzer Prize–winning *Of Thee I*

Sing, which opened in 1931. The huge lackluster building on your left is the Marriott Marquis. At the first set of bulb-lined arches, turn left into Shubert Alley and notice the silver-and-black images on the wall opposite the hotel's revolving doors. The mural depicts actors, singers, dancers, directors, choreographers, and scenes from *West Side Story, Cabaret, Hello Dolly, Peter Pan, Damn Yankees, Dancin', 42nd Street, A Chorus Line,* and *Ubee!* With the construction of the 49-story Marriott Marquis came the demolition of the Morosco, original Helen Hayes, Astor, Bijou, and Gaiety Theaters, and an outcry from the theater community. Some actors even threw themselves in front of bulldozers in an attempt to save the theater houses. Unfortunately, the hugely successful Marriott Marquis was an essential component of the neighborhood's economic revival. The glass elevator leading to the hotel's View Lounge on the top floor opens at 5PM and offers a good view of Times Square.

Turn right at the end of Shubert Alley to get back onto Seventh Avenue, and walk to the northeast corner of 46th Street and Times Square. The exterior of the 1929 shoe store in the Miller Building reads "The Show Folks Shoe Shop Dedicated to Beauty in Footwear." Shoemaker Israel Miller crafted ballet slippers for Broadway dancers and asked the public to vote for their favorite actresses. The winners, immortalized by sculptor Alexander Stirling Calder, are displayed from left to right: Ethyl Barrymore, Marilyn Miller, Mary Pickford, and Rosa Ponselle.

The church down the street, near Sixth Avenue, between Rosie O'Grady Restaurant and the Comfort Inn, is the Church of Saint Mary the Virgin, nicknamed "Smoky Mary's" because of its excessive use of incense. Built in 1895, this Episcopal church was the first to feature religious statues on its façade, which until then was antithetical to the American Puritan tradition. This started a trend of religious ornamentation on the exterior of churches in the country.

Back on Times Square, head uptown and you'll notice a TKTS booth selling half-price tickets on the island between Seventh Avenue and Broadway. Directly in front of the booth is a sculpture of Father Francis Patrick Duffy, a pastor at Church of the Holy Cross in the gritty Hell's Kitchen neighborhood from 1920 to 1932. Cross left to Broadway and continue uptown. On 49th Street, you'll find St. Malachy's Catholic Church on the north side of the street toward Eighth Avenue. Built in 1902, the "Actor's Chapel" was the place of worship for the entertainment community of the 1920s. Masses, confessions, and missions were arranged around theater schedules, and the cathedral was aglow with candles on opening nights.

Back on Broadway, between 49th and 50th Streets is the famous comedy club Caroline's on Broadway to your right and the Brill Building at 1619 Broadway to your left, which housed record companies, publishers, managers, artists, and promoters all under one roof.

When the original banker tenants pulled their money out of the building after the Great Depression, the owners were desperate for renters, and the building soon turned into an entertainment factory, nicknamed "Tin Pan Alley." Cole Porter, John Lennon, Eric Clapton, Paul Simon, Bob Dylan, Joni Mitchell, and Carly Simon have all recorded here, among many others. The gold bust above the door is thought to be building owner Abraham E. Lefcourt's son Alan, who died two years before the building was opened in 1931. The Winter Garden Theater, on the right side of the next block, ran *Cats* for eighteen years in a space that used to be a horse stable, and the Iridium Jazz Club next door is considered one of New York's major jazz clubs even though it has only been around since 1994.

At 53rd Street, glance up Broadway at the Ed Sullivan Theater, where David Letterman tapes his late show, and turn right. Follow 53rd Street all the way to Sixth Avenue. The large black building on the corner of 53rd Street is CBS Headquarters. On 53rd Street between Fifth and Sixth are the American Craft Museum and the **Museum of Modern Art (MoMA)**, which, with its reflective surface, is an anomaly among the brownstones on this block.

Continue on 53rd Street, crossing Fifth Avenue, past the waterfall on your left, and make a sharp left behind Burger Heaven. The graffiti sculpture before you is actually a piece of the Berlin Wall. Walk back to Fifth Avenue and continue making your way uptown. St. Thomas Church on the left side of 53rd Street is home to the nationally famous St. Thomas Boys' Choir, and the palatial Italian Renaissance–style building on the corner of 54th is the University Club, founded in 1865 to enable male graduates from different universities to socialize with each other (women were not admitted until 1987). Also on your left between 55th and 56th Streets is the Henri Bendel department store, in a townhouse with Lalique windows.

As you approach 57th Street, you'll see Tiffany's on your right. The clock hanging over the entrance has adorned every Tiffany store since 1853, and serves as a model for the desk clocks they make. Real New Yorkers know that you'll find a better selection of diamonds and jewelry for much lower prices ten blocks south in the Diamond District. Also on 57th Street is **Bergdorf Goodman**, with an unparalleled women's shoe department and an entirely separate store for their menswear. Continue to 58th Street and you'll find the **Plaza Hotel** to your left. Stop here to enjoy afternoon tea in the lobby with other New York visitors, or walk up Fifth Avenue three blocks to 61st Street to the Pierre's Rotunda Room for tea in a more intimate setting.

NEW YORK PUBLIC LIBRARY

The New York Public Library was the city's first public library at a time when the population was second only to London. The land was once a potter's field, or mass grave for hobos, prostitutes, and anyone else who didn't have a family to give them a proper burial. By 1842, the city decommissioned the graveyard and turned the space into the Croton Reservoir. The city reservoir was eventually moved to Central Park and the plot was filled with a marble library; in 1911 it was

the largest marble structure ever built in the nation's history. The original archive of books was donated by John Jacob Astor, the wealthiest man in the country at the time, whose private library was held in what is now the Joseph Papp Public Theater on Lafayette Street, and by James Lenox, whose collection was held on the site of the present-day Frick Collection on the Upper East Side. The merger of these two private collections, coupled with one-time governor Samuel J. Tilden's posthumous donation of $2.4 million, and a $9 million subsidy by the city, led to the 82-branch network the New York Public Library encompasses today, including tens of millions of literary materials, such as Jefferson's Declaration of Independence and the Gutenberg Bible. Note when looking at the building how all three major donors are inscribed into its marble façade.

BRYANT PARK

Bryant Park was built on the same potter's field as the New York Public Library. In the 1840s, with the construction of Croton Reservoir, Bryant Park was known as "Reservoir Square"—a place for high society to promenade. In 1853–1854 the very first world's fair took place in Bryant Park, featuring a "Crystal Palace"

structure made of iron and glass to house the industrial ware, consumer goods, and art exhibitions. The structure unfortunately burned down in 1858, and the park was renamed Bryant Park in 1884, in memory of the poet and newspaper editor William Cullen Bryant, who also strongly advocated the creation of Central Park. By the 1930s, the only purpose the park served was storage of construction equipment for the New York subway, but Parks Commissioner Robert Moses spearheaded a complete renovation of the space into the classical park design still evident today. In the 1960s, the park again devolved into an unsafe place, but by the late 1990s, park maintenance, warm-weather kiosks, and the number of events for the public increased, leading to a drastic decrease in crime rates. Currently, the park offers a summer film festival and live music and theatrical performances, and serves as a popular venue for functions. Interestingly, the park is entirely financed by private donors with no funding from the city at all.

TIMES SQUARE

Formerly "Longacre Square," this area became Times Square when the *New York Times* moved their offices here in 1904, at which point the Times Tower was the second tallest building in Manhattan. 1904 also marked the invention of neon lighting and the beginning of New York's subway system, all of which contributed to the neighborhood's heyday, which lasted until 1929. From 1914 to 1915, 43 theaters had put on 113 theatrical productions, and by 1927–1928, 264 shows had run on Broadway. The Great Depression forced many of the theaters to convert to burlesque shows and movie houses in the 1930s, but Rodgers and Hammerstein's collaboration on *Oklahoma!* helped revive the area in the 1940s. By the 1960s, the theater district became home to the pornography industry and erotic massage parlors, as portrayed in John Schlesinger's film *Midnight Cowboy*.

And by the 1970s and 1980s, not only was Times Square grimy, it was also the most dangerous neighborhood in New York City. In 1983, 2,300 crimes occurred on 42nd Street between Seventh and Eighth Avenues alone. Repeated attempts were made to clean up the neighborhood, but these attempts ironically made matters worse. Thinking that their buildings were about to be bulldozed, building owners didn't bother with maintenance or renovations.

The city lifted zoning restrictions on Times Square in order to lure developers, which is largely why the buildings in this area are so imposing and the sidewalks so seemingly devoid of space. In an attempt to create more light, the city required the ground levels to have neon signs, the brightness of which was measured by the Light Unit Times Square (LUTS). Today the neighborhood is extremely well lit, by the abundance of artificial light emanating from the prominent big-screen advertisements wrapped around the buildings.

One Times Square

The Times Building, housing the *New York Times*, officially opened on December 31, 1904. Until then, City Hall Park served as the city's gathering place on New Year's Eve. With the opening of the Times Building came a street party, fireworks, and a new tradition of New Year's in Times Square. The New Year's Eve "Ball," weighing 700 pounds and illuminated by 100 25-watt light bulbs, did not become a part of the festivities until 1907. It has commemorated New Year's Eve in Manhattan every year since, even after the New York Times left Times Tower in 1913 for its new home two blocks away on 43rd Street. The only years the ball wasn't in use were 1942 and 1943, when it was replaced by a moment of silence for World War II, followed by chimes ringing from Times Tower.

Throughout the 1980s, the ball took the form of a red "I love New York" apple, but the expensive bulbs were replaced by an LED display in the 1990s. As of the millennium, the ball has been covered in Waterford Crystal, and today is accompanied by one whole ton of confetti. The New Year's Eve ball is part of a nautical tradition of "time-balls" started in 1833 at England's Royal Observatory in Greenwich to synchronize its clock with the chronometers of nearby ships.

Sardi's

Sardi's opened in 1927 and quickly became the fashionable party venue after a Broadway show's opening. The owner, Vincent Sardi, kept his restaurant open later than any other in the area to accommodate his Broadway patrons, and if reviews were good, these patrons would be greeted with a standing ovation. A group called the "Cheese Club," composed of journalists, press agents, and theater critics, met for lunch here regularly, and the Tony Award was conceived here by friends of the late silent-film star Antoinette Perry. Today, Tony Award nominations (shortened from Antoinette) are announced in the restaurant, and the Outer Critics Circle Awards are presented here. 1,300 caricatures of celebrities adorn the walls, many of which were illustrated by Alex Gard, a Russian refugee who exchanged caricatures for meals until the day he died.

The Museum of Modern Art (MoMA)

Founded in 1929 through the joint efforts of the high-society champions of modernism Lillie P. Bliss, Mary Sullivan, and Abby Aldrich Rockefeller, this is one of the preeminent twentieth-century art museums in the world. Paintings and sculptures include the work of Pollack, Warhol, Dali, Kandinsky, and Picasso, and the museum also features cutting-edge photography and film exhibits. With its marble, tile, and glass façade, the MoMA was the first "international style" building in the country, as it was coined by museum builder Phillip Johnson at the MoMA exhibition in 1932.

The building was renovated and expanded to twice its original size by Japanese architect Yoshio Taniguchi in 2003. Unlike the preliminary version of the museum, which consisted of eight prints and one `drawing, today's MoMA holds 150,000 works of art. In addition to its art galleries, the museum also contains an education and research center, an auditorium, a sculpture garden, a reading room, an extensive library and archives, three cafés, and a bookstore.

Bergdorf Goodman

The setting in which Bergdorf Goodman is located was formerly the site of shipping and railroad mogul

Cornelius Vanderbilt's mansion. His home was one of the most decadent residences in the city's history until it was torn down in 1926. By 1928, an art deco clothing store had taken its place, run by Edwin Goodman, a former employer of immigrant tailor Herman Bergdorf. Goodman had been the first to introduce ready-to-wear garments at the request of one of his customers. Until then, all department stores had sales clerks that selected and custom designed items for the client to approve.

The seventh floor of the store, selling china, crystal, and home furnishings, is the most meticulously decorated in the building, and the only one with a restroom. The window right outside this "ladies' lounge" offers a spectacular view of the gardens in front of the Plaza Hotel, known as Grand Army Plaza, as well as of Central Park and the surrounding area. One floor up on the penthouse level is the John Barrett Salon, which honed the super-pale shade of blonde described in the 2004 beach read *Bergdorf Blondes* by Plum Sykes.

THE PLAZA

The Plaza is perhaps most famous for the 1950s series of *Eloise* books written by Kay Thompson, about a precocious six-year-old who lives at the hotel. The author, an eccentric singer, dancer, actress, and musical arranger, who herself lived at the Plaza for free for seven years, was rumored to have based the series on her goddaughter, Liza Minnelli. Apparently, Liza's antics while visiting Thompson included pouring Perrier down the mail chute, much like Eloise in the books. If you wander into the hotel, look for the Eloise painting at the far left side of the lobby.

When the Plaza Hotel opened in 1907, its Fifth Avenue promenade was considered the most fashionable area in the city. Known as Grand Army Plaza, the area serves as a tribute to the Union Army in the Civil War, evident by the equestrian statue of

Civil War hero General William Tecumseh Sherman. Newspaper publisher Joseph Pulitzer donated the Pulitzer Fountain that adorns the grassy section directly in front of this statue. The nineteen-story Plaza is no longer exclusively a hotel, with more than half of its rooms now residential; however, as the city's only hotel to be declared a national landmark, the exterior remains unaltered and afternoon tea continues to be served in the lobby's Palm Court.

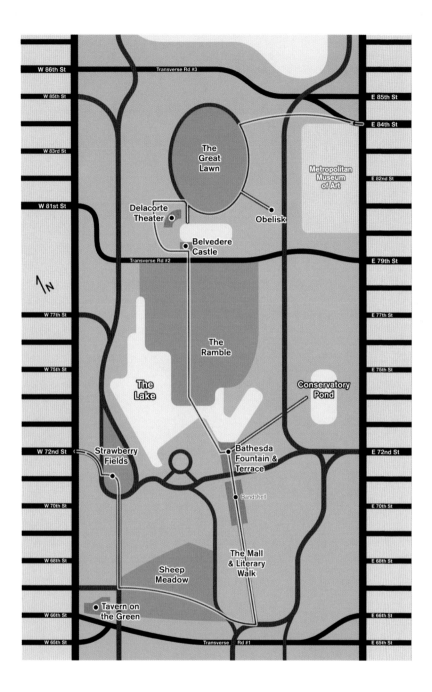

Central Park

*C*entral Park is the sprawling backyard for the 1.6 million inhabitants of Manhattan. It is the largest greenery in the city by far, stretching across 846 acres in total. Though it is meant to provide a natural recluse from Manhattan's electronic labyrinth, the park is entirely manmade down to its weeds. The two men responsible for its design are Frederick Law Olmsted (1822–1903), who crafted the landscape, and Calvert Vaux (1824–1895), who built the structures. In 1857, Olmsted and Vaux teamed up to enter the citywide design competition for a park, and submitted the winning entry, entitled the Greenswald Plan. The plan prioritized naturalistic elements over structural ones, and Vaux himself said "Nature first, second, and third— architecture after awhile."

The aim of the park was to compete with the open spaces of cosmopolitan cities like London and Paris where the wealthiest citizens could visibly display their affluence, inspiring the public to devote itself to hard work. The park still contains many elements of Olmsted and Vaux's initial design, such as carriage drives, riding trails, a principle fountain, and a fire watchtower, as well as new additions like playgrounds and the remodeled boathouse. The grasses get threadbare with use, but the space is a personal sanctuary filled with memories for many of the visitors who come here.

The Central Park Walk

Start:	Fifth Avenue and 84th Street
Finish:	72nd Street and Central Park West
Length:	2 miles
Time:	2 hours

Refreshments: Carts throughout the park sell beverages, pretzels, and ice cream.

Sights: Great Lawn, Obelisk, Belvedere Castle, Delacorte Theater, the "Ramble," Bow Bridge, Bethesda Fountain, Lake, Loeb Boathouse, Bethesda Terrace, Model Boat Pond, Naumberg Bandshell, Mall Literary Walk, Sheep Meadow, Tavern on the Green, Strawberry Fields

Note: Many of the activities that take place year round are listed at www.centralpark.com\pages\activities.html.

Enter the park at Fifth Avenue and 84th Street, at the north side of the Metropolitan Museum of Art. To the left you'll see the glass gallery of the museum's Egyptian wing, as well as large rocks of Manhattan schist sticking out of the ground. Vaux initially tried to keep the museum out of the park, but when he realized he was fighting a losing battle, he decided to design the museum building with an entrance that led into the park. The main entrance to the museum was later moved to Fifth Avenue and the original façade is now displayed in the museum's American wing. You'll soon come to the main park Loop, where traffic consists solely of bicyclists, rollerbladers, and runners. The full Loop is 6.2 miles, and New York City marathoners run by this spot at their 25th mile of the race. Cross the Loop carefully and continue straight to the walking path on the other side. You'll come to the immense **Great Lawn**, which is right in the middle of the park.

Turn left on the hexagonal tiles and count six streetlamps down until you get to a paved path on the left. Bear right on this path until you see the 71-foot **Obelisk**. Once you've taken it in, descend the steps facing the front of the Obelisk and turn left, and make a right back toward the Great Lawn.

Back at the Great Lawn, make a left and follow the tiled path until you see Belvedere Castle, with an American flag on top. Make a left on the path that leads to the "Dragonfly Preserve" sign. You'll see a dock that provides a view of the castle and the pond surrounding it. Retrace your steps back to the main walkway and make a left. You'll pass the Delacorte Theater on your left and a small stone building with a rich history that now serves as a women's public restroom. Olmsted imported this stone structure in 1877 from Fairmount Park, Pennsylvania, where it was designed as a schoolhouse for the 1876 World's Fair Centennial Exhibition. The house was later used as the head-quarters for the park's Swedish Cottage Marionette Theater. The Delacorte Theater behind it, donated by Dell Comics founder George T. Delacorte, is the performance space for "Shakespeare in the Park," a free public event starring high-profile actors, such as Meryl Streep, Kevin Kline, and Phillip Seymour Hoffman.

Make a left past the restroom and continue straight until you come to a set of steps to **Belvedere Castle**. Once you climb these steps, you'll have a great view of the theater, and if you enter the castle and go upstairs, you'll have a terrific view of the park as well. The area to the north of Delacorte Theater stretching west to the Museum of Natural History was known as Seneca Village, which was once home to the largest community of free blacks in the country before they were displaced by park developers.

When leaving Belvedere Castle, take the seven wide steps down, and walk straight until you see a sign for the **"Ramble."** Follow the Ramble straight down. The path narrows after awhile and you will come to a fork. Either path will lead you to a small bridge over a stream. Cross the bridge and continue along the path until you reach the bigger Bow Bridge. If it's warm out you'll see rowboaters on either side of you. Named for its resemblance to an archer's bow, Bow Bridge is one of nine original park bridges, seven of which still remain. It was built between 1859 and 1862, and connects the Ramble and Cherry Hill. To the right of the bridge is a phenomenal view of the Upper West Side skyline. Ice-skating was very popular on this artificial 22-acre lake in the 1800s because it allowed for physical contact that would otherwise be inappropriate. Skaters could bump into each other and hold hands, and women were expected to hike their skirts over their ankles for greater mobility.

When you get to the other side of the bridge, continue straight until you get to the **Bethesda Fountain**. Across the **Lake** to your left is the Loeb Boathouse. Once a deteriorating wooden boathouse, this brick Loeb Boathouse has stood here since March 1954, when Parks Commissioner Robert Moses encouraged Adeline and Carl M. Loeb to fund its renovation. The restaurant serves as the unofficial headquarters of the Central Park birdwatchers, who record their sightings in a notebook inside. The stairs and tunnels to your right comprise the Bethesda Terrace. Jacob Wrey Mould was the British architect who designed the ornamentation around the park, such as the various wildlife and seasonal carvings on the terrace's exterior. The terrace also has 16,000 colored tiles lining its interior.

Take the path closest to the Lake so that you see the weeping willows and the lake on your left. You'll come to a tunnel at the bottom of a set of steps, known as Trefoil Arch. Go through the tunnel, make a left and then a right, and you'll come to the **Model Boat Pond**. Walk back toward the tunnel, which you'll now see has three lobes like a shamrock (hence the name "trefoil") and turn left before continuing through, so that you're at the main park Loop.

Cross at the light and follow the Loop in the direction of traffic until you get to the top of the steps leading to Bethesda Fountain. Instead of going down the steps, turn left, cross the street and walk straight. You'll see the Naumberg Bandshell on your left, where Wednesday and Saturday band concerts were once a popular feature of park life. Get onto the wide promenade, or the **Mall**, where park-goers would come to see and be seen. Olmsted and Vaux loved the canopy effect of American elms, and so lined the walkway with double rows of these rare trees on either side. The south end of the Mall contains the Olmsted Flower Bed, which is a small memorial garden surrounded by American elms, presented on what would have been Olmsted's 150th birthday. This is the only tribute to Olmsted in the entire park. Eventually you will come to statues of great literary and historical figures. The first one on your left is Fitz-Greene Halleck. You'll then see Sir Walter Scott, Robert Burns, as well as Christopher Columbus and William Shakespeare farther down. This is the **Literary Walk**. The paving stones on the ground commemorate trees endowed throughout the park. Behind Christopher Columbus is the fenced-in **Sheep Meadow**. If you walk straight across it, which can be difficult on a beautiful summer day because of its densely populated grass, you'll come to **Tavern on the Green** across the street.

Turn right and walk up the road until you come to a statue of Daniel Webster on the equivalent of West 71st Street. Cross the loop to enter **Strawberry Fields**, the elevated garden reserved for quiet recreation. You'll see the famous mosaic "Imagine" plaque, which was placed directly across the street from the Dakota, where John Lennon was shot.

THE GREAT LAWN

This oval space was a reservoir until the city drained it and turned it into a grassy region in 1937, at which point it became a popular performance venue. Elton John, Diana Ross, Paul Simon, and Pope John Paul II have all drawn large crowds here, but since the 1980s, when it was nicknamed the "Great Dustbowl," only 8 events are held here annually. Thanks to the Central Park Conservancy, the grass is as lush as ever, and on warm days the area is populated with sunbathers and schoolchildren. The Metropolitan Opera and the New York Philharmonic each give two sunset performances here a summer, which fill the park with uncharacteristically tranquil New Yorkers on blankets.

THE OBELISK (OR "CLEOPATRA'S NEEDLE")

The Obelisk is by far the oldest structure in the park. It is one of a pair commissioned by Thutmosis III in 1600 BCE for the entrance to the Temple of Tum in Heliopolis, Egypt. For over 1,000 years they stood covered in dazzling electrum (a gold and silver alloy used for jewelry) reflecting the sun's light, until the Persian conqueror Cambyses ordered them to be laid down. For centuries the obelisks lay in the dust, until Caesar heard about them and brought them to Alexandria to adorn his Caesarium temple, which commemorated the Roman conquest of Egypt. He had one placed before the very structure where Cleopatra and Marc Antony were lovers, which is why it is known today as "Cleopatra's Needle."

After the American Civil War, the khedive of Egypt offered the artifact to the United States as a gift. He hoped that this gesture would stimulate Egyptian-American relations, and in particular open New York's harbor to the Egyptian cotton trade, since the abolition of slavery had recently halted the cotton industry in the South. William H. Vanderbilt took care of the $100,000 shipping and handling costs, and his friend Lt. Commander Henry Honeychurch Gorringe contracted, negotiated, and physically transported the Obelisk to New York.

When Gorringe first arrived in Alexandria to pick up the Obelisk, it had become the main attraction of a proposed luxury housing project, and the only way he could get it out of the city was to sneak it ten miles by water instead of one mile by land through the back streets as he had originally intended. No Egyptian seaman would agree to work on a ship with the Obelisk on board, so Gorringe imported a Yugoslav crew, and soon learned that not a single member spoke any language besides Serbo-Croatian, and that none had ever been to sea. Gorringe was nevertheless determined, and in 1881 his ship reached the Hudson River. It took four months just to move the Obelisk from the Hudson River to the park by rollers and a donkey engine. During its assembly in Central Park, Gorringe hid a lead time capsule between the foundation stones. The capsule contains documents, records, obelisk data, coins and medals, the Bible, the works of William Shakespeare, a dictionary, and samples of various tools in common use at the time.

After all of Gorringe's efforts, he netted only $1,156 and died in an accident three years later. The Obelisk has also suffered more damage in its few short decades in New York than it had in centuries, as is evident by the faded hieroglyphics, which have all but vanished. The crowd at the 1881 installation ceremony numbered 10,000, but in recent times the Obelisk is an oft-neglected site in a quiet nook of the park.

BELVEDERE CASTLE

Belvedere Castle (meaning "beautiful view" in Italian) is constructed out of the Manhattan schist that comprises its base. Designed by Calvert Vaux in 1867, the Victorian Gothic castle-like building is meant to create the impression that it is rising organically from the rocks. Originally the castle overlooked a reservoir, until the reservoir turned into the Great Lawn in 1937. Vaux didn't want the castle to dominate the landscape, but rather act as a scenic accent within it, and as such it sits partly hidden from the park, contributing more to the set of the Delacorte Theater than to the Great Lawn. Vaux also didn't want the castle to have doors or windows, hoping that years of water damage would cause the castle to collapse and appear more romantic, but doors were added in 1919, and the Central Park Conservancy fully restored the structure in 1983 and has maintained it ever since. Originally a fire watchtower, the castle became the New York meteorological observatory in 1868 and housed offices for the United States Weather Bureau in 1919. Today, meteorological instruments are automated, but whenever the temperature in Central Park is reported on the news, it is still measured from this point.

The Ramble

The Ramble was the first area of the park's landscape to be completed. It consists of 38 acres of completely artificial gardens "in the wild," with even a water tap controlling the babbling stream. Olmsted designed the ramble to be an unruly sanctuary from Manhattan's deliberate grid where visitors could ramble aimlessly (hence the name) through a natural setting. Due to its topography and placement on the Atlantic bird migration route, the Ramble is considered one of the 15 best bird watching sites in the United States. 250 species of birds have been spotted here, and during the spring and fall the area teems with twenty species of warbler alone that rest here during their migrations.

Bethesda Fountain

This world-famous fountain named *Angel of the Waters* is the only sculpture that was planned in the initial design of the park and the only statue in the park created by a female sculptor. Emma Stebbins (1815–1882) designed the statue in Rome in 1861 and completed it seven years later. Her brother was Henry G. Stebbins, who was Central Park's commissioner at the time.

The fountain was dedicated at the opening of the Croton Aqueduct in 1842, which brought much-needed fresh water from Westchester into the city. In the original Pool of Bethesda in Jerusalem, the sick would gather and wait for angels to trouble the water in order to be cured of their diseases. Stebbins designed the fountain as a tribute to both the restorative powers of the biblical fountain and the revitalizing water that the new aqueduct supplied.

At a height of 26 feet, Bethesda Fountain is one of the largest fountains in New York. The neoclassical winged figure symbolizes the integrity of the city's water supply, with a purifying lily in one hand and an outstretched arm blessing the water below. The cherubs surrounding the basin represent Peace, Purity, Temperance, and Health. In the 1960s and 1970s, the fountain was a major hippie hangout and gained the nickname "the Freak Fountain."

The Model Boat Pond
(or Conservatory Water)

This space was originally designed as a conservatory with ornamental flowerbeds, but the flower parterre was turned into an ornamental pond instead. Model-boat racing became so popular on the Conservatory Water that the pond is now known as the Model Boat Pond.

Surrounding the pond is a statue of Hans Christian Andersen, reading "The Ugly Duckling" to a bronze duckling, as well as an Alice in Wonderland statue complete with the Cheshire Cat, Mad Hatter, and Dormouse. For generations children have climbed this enormous statue, commissioned in 1959 by George T. Delacorte in honor of his wife. Supposedly the Mad Hatter has Delacorte's face.

From the Model Boat Pond, if you look east to 927 Fifth Avenue, on the twelfth floor you can see the nest of two red-tailed hawks named Pale Male and Lola. The coop board of the building once evicted these famous hawks after they had been there living there for ten years. For weeks residents of the building and the neighborhood vociferously protested this move until the board finally conceded and installed a structure to support a new nest. Within weeks Pale Male and Lola had rebuilt their home. The hawks are often seen flying around the park.

LITERARY WALK

The Literary Walk exemplifies Olmsted and Vaux's attempt to have the park resemble a landscape painting. Though they were determined to keep "artificial objects" out of the park, various literary and nonliterary figures have come to inhabit this walkway, giving it its name. Besides the obvious concern that the statuary would interference with the park's organic setting, there was another concern that the notable people of the time, memorialized in sculpture, would be irrelevant and obscure at a later date. This is precisely what happened to the poet Fitz-Greene Halleck, who was memorialized in 1870 with even President Rutherford B. Hayes attending the inception, but is completely unknown today. The statue of Christopher Columbus is one of two in the city, the other standing in Columbus Circle. Both Italians and Spaniards claim him, so the Spanish Columbus lives in the park and the Italian Columbus resides in Columbus Circle.

Sheep Meadow

The designers intended this 15-acre field to be a parade ground, but the city feared that the Civil War militia would destroy it with their recklessness, so they banned parades before the first one was ever held. By the 1930s, this area became a literal sheep meadow, where sheep roamed twice a day. Tavern on the Green served as the sheepfold (where the sheep lived). By 1978, the meadow was barely green because of the many demonstrations in the 1960s, including one in which Martin Luther King spoke. Currently, there are strict limitations on the meadow's uses: demonstrations and concerts are prohibited, as are animals, and, rather bizarrely, keeping score on games.

Tavern on the Green

In 1934, Parks Commissioner Robert Moses removed the sheep from the park, and the 1871 Victorian Gothic sheepfold became the notoriously overpriced Tavern on the Green restaurant. The playground across from the restaurant was another feature of the park that Moses wanted to bulldoze in the 1960s, but he came up against some very strong opposition. During the preliminary planning stages, a member of the construction crew left blueprints on a park bench, which an Upper West Side mother found. She immediately sprung into action, rallying the neighborhood moms and the local press. The "Battle of Central Park" ensued, involving a group of mothers with strollers physically blocking bulldozers from demolishing their children's playground. When Moses lost this battle, he was said to have forfeited not only his parking lot that day, but also his reputation. A prominent and popular figure until the late 1960s, his reign ended at this playground and he gave up reshaping Central Park for good.

STRAWBERRY FIELDS

Yoko Ono donated $1 million to the Central Park Conservancy to create and maintain the 2.5-acre section of the park known as Strawberry Fields. If you view the area from above, you'll notice that landscape architect Bruce Kelly designed the grassy tribute in the shape of a tear. The park dedicated the area in 1985 on Lennon's birthday, five years after his assassination, and named it after the Beatles song "Strawberry Fields Forever," which Lennon composed about his Liverpool childhood. Strawberry Fields was the name of a Salvation Army reformatory where Lennon and his friends used to go to garden parties and play when they were young. At the time, Lennon's aunt Mimi didn't want him to get involved with a questionable element of children, but Lennon reassured her, "What are they gonna do, hang me?" which is supposedly where the line "nothing to get hung about" comes from.

Birds have eaten the strawberries, but the area contains 121 unique species of shrub for the 121 countries that existed at the time. The black-and-white mosaic "Imagine" plaque near the west entrance is the only reference to John Lennon in Strawberry

Fields. There are almost always flowers, candles, or poems placed on this spot in remembrance of the musician, and even the mosaic itself, which is made out of Italian marble, was donated as a gift by Neapolitan craftsmen. The original Strawberry Fields was a place where Lennon could be alone and free with his thoughts, and today the Central Park version serves the same purpose for its visitors.

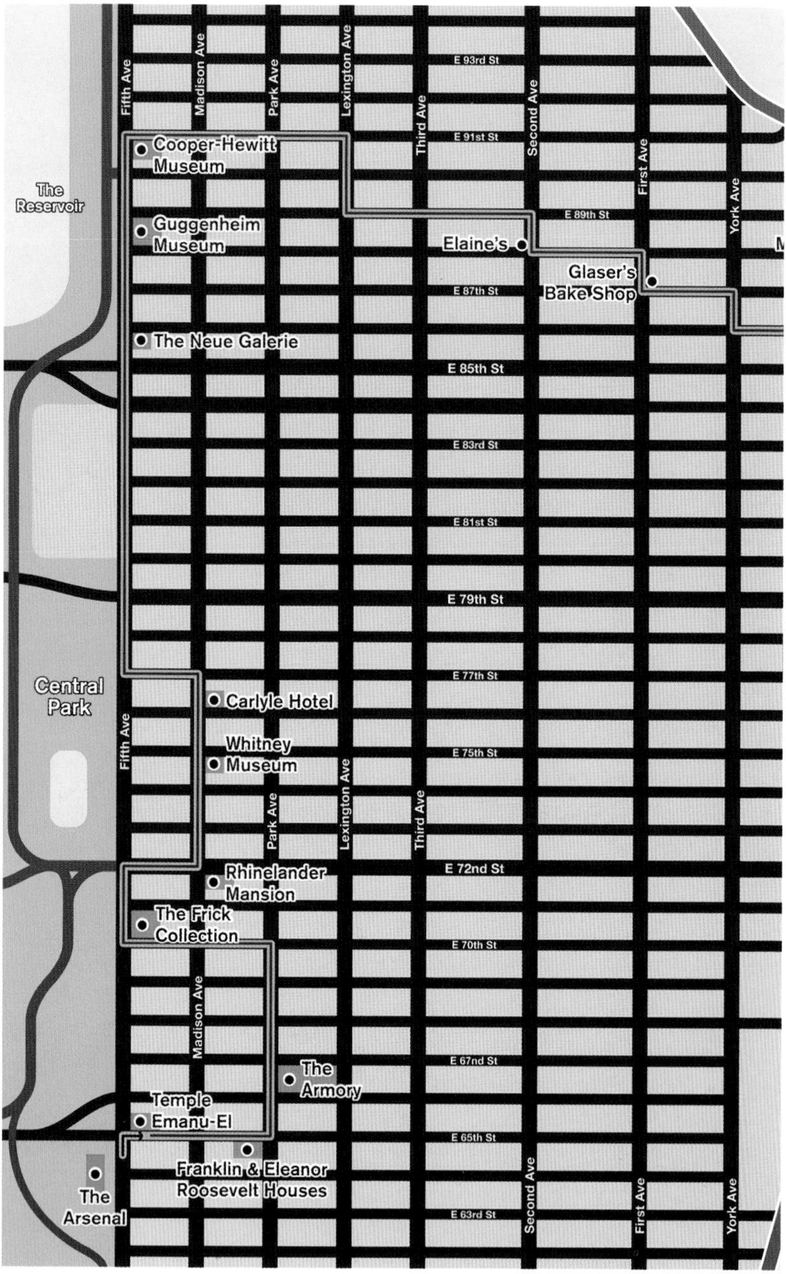

Fifth Ave
Madison Ave
Park Ave
Lexington Ave
Third Ave
Second Ave
First Ave
York Ave
E 93rd St
E 91st St
E 89th St
E 87th St
E 85th St
E 83rd St
E 81st St
E 79th St
E 77th St
E 75th St
E 72nd St
E 70th St
E 67nd St
E 65th St
E 63rd St
The Reservoir
Central Park
Cooper-Hewitt Museum
Guggenheim Museum
The Neue Galerie
Elaine's
Glaser's Bake Shop
Carlyle Hotel
Whitney Museum
Rhinelander Mansion
The Frick Collection
The Armory
Temple Emanu-El
Franklin & Eleanor Roosevelt Houses
The Arsenal

Upper East Side

As you walk around the Upper East Side, you'll see doormen hailing taxis, private school children clustered on street corners, and the largest concentration of nail salons in the city. A predominantly residential neighborhood, the Upper East Side encompasses Fifth Avenue and Park Avenue, the two most expensive streets in Manhattan, so it is no surprise that the 10021 zip code is among the most affluent in the country. Fifth Avenue overlooks Central Park and Park Avenue overlooks the grassy flowerbeds that sit directly above the Metro-North Railroad tunnel, while Madison Avenue is known for its high-end shopping, Lexington Avenue for its chain stores, and the streets further east for their family-friendly high-rises.

The neighborhood also has an abundance of religious institutions, and you'll almost always be within eyeshot of a church, mosque, or synagogue. The most distinctive aspect of the neighborhood however, is the wealth of museums stretching between 82nd and 105th Streets on Fifth Avenue, known as Museum Mile. If you stroll along these streets, you'll see not only extensive artwork, but exquisite architecture as well. Every summer at the Museum Mile Festival, the sidewalks are blocked off for music and art performances and admission to all museums is free.

The Upper East Side Walk

Start:	Fifth Avenue and 64th Street
Finish:	Carl Schurz Park on 86th Street and the East River
Length:	2.5 miles
Time:	2 hours

Refreshments: Serendipity 3, if you're with small children and for the desserts and décor; La Goulue for people-watching on Madison Avenue; E.A.T. for gourmet salads and sandwiches you can either eat inside or take to Central Park; Jackson Hole for burgers and mozzarella sticks; Sarabeth's for brunch or tea.

Sights: Central Park Zoo, Temple Emanu-El, Franklin and Eleanor Roosevelt Houses, Asia Society Museum, 740 Park Avenue, the Frick Collection, the Rhinelander Mansion, Whitney Museum of American Art, Hotel Carlyle, Metropolitan Museum of Art, the Guggenheim, Cooper Hewitt National Design Museum, Church of the Holy Trinity, Elaine's, Glaser's Bake Shop, Henderson Place, Carl Schurz Park, Gracie Mansion, East River.

At Fifth Avenue and 64th Street, you'll see a magnificent entrance to the **Central Park Zoo**. The ivy-covered 1848 Civil War bunkhouse known as "the Arsenal" now serves as the zoo's administrative offices, but this building also housed the American Museum of Natural History from 1869 to 1877. Currently, the second floor is a public library and the conference room holds Frederick Law Olmsted and Calvert Vaux's original Greenwald Plan for Central Park.

Continue up Fifth Avenue and look for **Temple Emanu-El** to your right on 65th Street. Note the art deco touches on the 1929 building, such as the stylized lions above the high arch and the three-dimensional ornamentation. Continue east on 65th Street, past Madison Avenue to the middle of the next block. At

47 East 65th Street, you'll come to the Sara Delano Roosevelt and Franklin and Eleanor Roosevelt Houses, now a division of Hunter College. This is the house FDR lived in while recovering from polio from 1921 to 1922, and his home when he won the presidential election in 1932. This is also the venue where Eleanor Roosevelt held civic and political meetings throughout her career serving the public. Daniel, one of the most expensive restaurants in the city, serves upscale French cuisine across the street.

Turn left on Park Avenue and look for the large brick Seventh Regiment Armory on your right, in the middle of the next block. Members of this regiment fought in every American war since the country's founding, but Manhattanites know the space best for its annual antiques show. The pedestrian bridge to your right is part of Hunter College. The design firm of McKim, Mead and White built the 1911 Percy Rivington Pyne House on the northwest corner of 68th Street, named for its former English owner. The house served as a design template for many other buildings on Park Avenue and housed the Soviet Mission to the United States from 1948 to 1963. Nearby is the Americas Society, an organization that promotes an understanding of the Americas through artistic expression. The Spanish Institute and the Instituto Italiano di Cultura sit next door, followed by the Italian Consulate. The 1932 Union Club on the northeast corner of Park Avenue was built to house New York's biggest club.

Continue up Park Avenue to 70th Street and you'll come to the modern **Asia Society Museum**. The garden on the south side of the building is part of the Garden Court Café. Glance diagonally across the street at the tiered 740 Park Avenue on the northwest corner of 71st Street. This building is the single most expensive building in New York City, with a history as rich as its residents, which have included real-estate magnate John D. Rockefeller, Jr., ITT International CEO Rand V. Araskog, Warner Communications CEO Steven Ross Stroll, Revlon CEO Ron Perelman, and former First Lady Jacqueline Bouvier. Walk east on 70th Street to Lexington Avenue and back, taking in the unique townhouses, like the one housing Salon Visentin at 131 East 70th Street, which architect Grosvenor Atterbury remodeled in 1911. Atterbury designed the original Whitney Museum and the American wing of the Metropolitan Museum of Art. Also look at 125 East 70th Street, financier Paul Mellon's 1966 yellow stucco house, guarded by a suburban-style wall.

Walk back west on 70th Street, past Estée Lauder's home on 45 East 70th Street between Park and Madison, and look for the Explorer's Club across the street at 46 East 70th Street, founded in 1904 to promote the scientific exploration of land, sea, air, and space. You'll soon come to the charming courtyard of the **Frick Collection** on your right. Exiting the Frick, walk up to 72nd Street and turn right. The elaborate, columned 1894 buildings on the north side of the street comprised the Lycée Francais de New York grammar and high schools for 38 years. The buildings are occasionally still referred to by their nineteenth-century owners: National Fuel Gas Company director Oliver Gould Jennings, who owned the house on the left, and furniture magnate Henry T. Sloane, who owned the house on the right. The Lycée moved from this location in the fall of 2002 and the buildings have since been reconverted to private residences.

Another magnificent turn-of-the-century mansion awaits you at 867 Madison Avenue on the corner of 72nd Street, in the form of the Ralph Lauren flagship store, known formally as the Rhinelander Mansion. The Rhinelanders never actually moved into their mansion, perhaps because Mr. Rhinelander died before the building was completed. From 1898 to 1921 the house was empty, and it served as a residential and commercial space until Ralph Lauren took it over in 1984. The interior of the store is furnished lavishly, with one of the largest handcrafted staircases in the country, on which a symphony quartet performs in the Christmas season, and windows made of Lalique glass panels from the original Polo Lounge at the Beverly Hills Hotel.

Continue up Madison Avenue, past the Madison Avenue Presbyterian Church on 73rd Street, which sits on part of the 30-acre land once owned by Robert Lenox, one of the five wealthiest men in New York at the time of his death in 1840. You'll soon come to the **Whitney Museum of American Art** on 75th Street. When you leave the Whitney, continue up Madison Avenue to **Hotel Carlyle**. The tower, modeled after Westminster Cathedral in London, emanates a green glow to the Upper East Side skyline at dusk.

Turn left on 77th Street and walk past the Mark Hotel to get back on Fifth Avenue. Walking up Fifth, you'll come to the New York University Institute of Fine Arts and the small Florence Gould Garden next door. American Tobacco Company founder James B. Duke built this mansion in 1912, and the family donated it to New York University in 1957. You'll also pass the Payne Whitney House, named for the wealthy lawyer who once lived here with his family, and the ornate entrance of the French Embassy. These low-rise buildings are anomalies on Fifth Avenue, which mostly contains prewar high-rises. At the corner of 79th Street, you'll come to the 1897–1899 Fletcher Sinclair House, named for the founder of the Sinclair Oil and Refining Company.

Keep walking up Fifth Avenue until you see the four blocks spanning the **Metropolitan Museum of Art**. In warmer months, street vendors line these blocks, selling prints, handmade jewelry, and T-shirts. At 86th Street, look out for the red brick Neue Galerie on the corner to your left, exhibiting German and Austrian art. Then walk to 88th Street, where you'll stumble onto a large cinnamon bun of a building, known as the **Guggenheim**. 89th Street is named "Fred Lebow Place" for the Romanian director of the New York City

Marathon from 1970 to 1993. He died of brain cancer in 1994 after completing 69 marathons in his lifetime. The "Runner's Gate" across 90th Street leads to the Central Park Reservoir and the last leg of the New York City Marathon. Look for the National Academy Museum between 89th and 90th Streets and the Episcopal Church of the Heavenly Rest on 90th and Fifth Avenue, founded by a group of Civil War veterans. The magnificent grounds of **Cooper Hewitt National Design Museum** sit between 90th and 91st Streets on Fifth Avenue.

Turn right on 91st Street to come to a row of private elementary schools educating New York City's miniature elite. The 1918 limestone building directly across from Cooper Hewitt is the Convent of the Sacred Heart, New York's first independent girls' school, and formerly the Otto and Addie Kahn mansion, named for the railroad financier who funded the Metropolitan Opera Company. The mansion's unusual design was modeled after the fifteenth-century Palazzo della Cancelleria in Rome. You'll see the Russian Consulate nearby, as well as the all-girls' Spence School.

Cross Madison Avenue and continue on 91st Street, where you'll pass Dalton's elementary school. On the corner of 91st and Park Avenue is the Presbyterian Brick Church. As you approach Lexington Avenue, you'll come to 128 East 91st Street, the secret Addiction Recovery Institute (ARI) frequented by the likes of Rush Limbaugh. On Lexington Avenue, diagonally across from you, stands the 92nd Street Y, founded by German Jews in 1874 but open to all ethnicities and faiths.

Head down Lexington and look for Weitz, Weitz & Coleman to your left in the middle of the next block, a rare-book and book-binding business that has been around since 1909. At 89th Street, turn left and notice the handful of three-story Queen Anne houses that remain on the block. Continue down 89th Street to Second Avenue, turn right, and walk toward the big yellow "Elaine's" sign. In Woody Allen's 1979 film *Manhattan*, this long-standing literary hangout is where the characters convene at the beginning of the movie to discuss art and life. Woody Allen, appropriately, lives in the neighborhood.

Make a left on 88th Street and continue east, passing the French Gothic Church of the Holy Trinity, with a flower garden that provides a setting for classical music concerts on summer evenings. Make another right onto First Avenue and look for Glaser's Bake Shop, opened by German immigrant John Glaser in 1902. You might be able to resist the aroma of fresh baked goods from the outside, but if you step inside your resistance will be shot.

Turn left onto 87th Street, passing the former orphanage known as St. Joseph's Catholic Church and School. The parish traditionally served a German-speaking congregation, due to the high number of German families that lived in this neighborhood in the late nineteenth century. Make another right on York Avenue and a left onto 86th Street.

Continue east until you see the alley on your left called Henderson Place, built by the wealthy fur hat salesman John C. Henderson in 1882. The entrance to **Carl Schurz Park** is directly ahead of you on East End Avenue. Walk straight and ascend the curved stone staircase for an unobstructed view of the East River. Then turn left and walk in the uptown direction until you get to the northern tip of the park, from where the *Yankee Clipper* ferry departs to Yankee Stadium. Look to your right for a view of Gracie Mansion, the residence of every New York mayor, except Mike Bloomberg, since Fiorello LaGuardia in 1942. Scottish shipping magnate Archibald Gracie built the mansion in 1798, and this is where he entertained such distinguished guests as John Quincy Adams and Louis Philippe, before Adams became the president of the United States and Philippe the king of France. The city acquired the mansion in 1891 and used the property as the Museum of the City of New York before designating it the mayor's residence. Follow the path all the way around the mansion for glimpses into its charming rooms. The esplanade offers benches for weary legs and a serene waterside stroll for those who wish to walk along the path.

CENTRAL PARK ZOO

The southern part of Central Park has long housed animals in its simulated unruly habitat. As early as the 1860s, a number of white swans and a black bear cub roamed this part of the park. By 1934 Parks Commissioner Robert Moses started a zoo, but the facility could not keep up with the abundance of animals. The zoo was renovated in the 1980s and expanded to five acres. It was one of the first urban zoos to have natural environments for animals instead of cages. 130 different species inhabit the zoo today, including the polar bears, foxes, penguins, and seals in the Polar Zone, the monkeys, birds, and reptiles in the Tropic Zone and the sea lions, red pandas, otters, and geese in the Temperate Territory. The zoo also plays a role in the protection and preservation of several endangered species.

TEMPLE EMANU-EL

Built on the site of John Jacob Astor's mansion in the 1920s, Temple Emanu-El was New York's first reformed Jewish congregation. Rabbi Samuel Adler led the 33-member German immigrant congregation in 1845. His son Felix later started the New York Society for Ethical Culture on the Upper West Side in 1876. Congregation Emanu-El met on the Lower East Side until moving into this building in 1929, after merging with the reform institution Beth-El. If you look to the right of the temple you'll see the original entrance for Temple Beth-El. The building itself, which was designed by two architectural firms to incorporate art deco influences while maintaining the Jewish tradition, is the largest Jewish house of worship in the world. With a 10-story vaulted roof and seating for 2,500 people, the *New York Times* once dubbed the synagogue "the Little Cathedral."

Every stained-glass window over the main entrance is symbolic. The seven windows at the very top symbolize the seven days of creation and/or the seven branches of the menorah lamp. The twelve-piece wheel represents the twelve tribes of Israel, and they surround the Magen David, or six-pointed star. The four arched columns of nine windows represent the 4,000 years of Jewish history that have passed, and the 36 interior windows represent the 36 righteous people thought to exist in every generation. The eighteen panes of glass around the interior of the central arch symbolize the eighteen benedictions of standing prayer, and also represent *chai*, the Hebrew word for life. A small museum in the temple contains antique lamps, Torah ornaments, and memorabilia.

Asia Society Museum

Founded in 1956 by John D. Rockefeller III, the Asia Society is one of a network of nonprofit organizations around the world established to strengthen the relationship between the United States and the Asia-Pacific region. The society offers performances, lectures, films, and art exhibitions, and features 300 works of art dating back to 2000 BCE from the Rockefellers' private collection. The organization has been in this building since 1981. Asia Society's symbol is the leogryph, a mythical beast that is part-lion and part-griffin, generally found at the entrance to Buddhist temples, symbolizing protection against evil. Currently, two bronze leogryphs guard eighth-floor elevators.

The Frick Collection

December 16, 1935, marked the first day Pittsburgh coke and steel millionaire Henry Clay Frick's private art collection was open to the public. Until this time, the $50 million collection and mansion that housed it was

only accessible to Frick's family and close friends. Frick had always secretly planned to bequeath the house and its contents, ranging from Renaissance to late-nineteenth-century art, to the public, but his architects had designed the space as a private residence.

The museum still resembles the mansion that Frick and his family lived in from 1914 to 1919, complete with period furniture and rooms with names like the Living Hall, where Mr. Frick chatted with his male guests in front of a fireplace, and Fragonard Room, where Mrs. Frick entertained her female guests against a backdrop of eighteenth-century French artist Jean-Honoré Fragonard's paintings, stretching from floor to ceiling. Other celebrated artists represented in the collection include Goya, El Greco, Rembrandt, and Renoir. The most arresting room, considering that the residence is located in the middle of a bustling city, is the Garden Court. This indoor courtyard is illuminated by a skylight and contains an indoor pond with a fountain. Back when the Fricks lived here, the court served as a driveway leading to the building's main entrance. After National Gallery architect John Russell Pope converted the driveway into a courtyard during the building's remodeling, many other museums emulated the design of galleries surrounding a central courtyard.

Not all of the Frick Collection's rooms are accessible to the public; Mr. Frick's private game room in the basement contains a two-lane bowling alley and billiards table that is only rarely used for museum functions.

The Metropolitan Museum of Art

The Metropolitan Museum of Art is a world unto itself. Initially designed by Calvert Vaux and Jacob Wrey Mould, two of the artistic minds behind Central Park, the museum has become the largest and widest ranging in the western hemisphere. The museum was founded in 1870 by a group of Civil War Union sympathizers, philanthropists, and artists, including lawyers John Jay and Joseph H. Choate, and poet William Cullen Bryant. Its first noteworthy collection consisted of 174 Dutch and Flemish paintings. When wealthy financier J.P. Morgan served as president from 1904 to 1913, he expanded the museum substantially, both with his own art collection and through his funding of new acquisitions and archeological excavations. Known for its Egyptian, African, American, Asian, Byzantine, Oceanic, and Middle Eastern art, as well as its collection of European masterpieces, for much of the twentieth century the museum refused to acknowledge abstraction as an art form. However, today all types of art are exhibited in this massive space, ranging from Van Gogh to Rauschenberg.

The architectural additions to the Met over the years have made the museum seem more like a series of smaller art collections within a larger structure than one cohesive exhibition space. Within these smaller pockets lie period rooms that replicate the originals so accurately that they elicit a feeling of time travel. Among these hidden gems is the Astor Court with its Chinese landscaping, modeled on a Ming dynasty (1368–1644) scholar's courtyard; the Swiss Room with its carved and veneered panels and ceiling, built to recreate a 1682 home in an Alpine village of eastern Switzerland; the 1707 Nur al-Din Room from

Damascus, Syria, with colorful marble floors, a fountain, Arabic inscriptions, and high stained-glass windows; and the inviting Frank Lloyd Wright Room, designed in 1912–1914 as a living room for the Francis W. Little House in Wayzata, Minnesota. As you wander through the museum, be sure to also check out the Temple of Dendur in the Egyptian wing and the Cantor Rooftop Garden, offering outdoor sculpture and an ample view of the city.

The Whitney Museum of American Art

Founded by Gertrude Vanderbilt Whitney in 1930, the Whitney was the first museum dedicated to twentieth-century American art. Whitney herself was a sculptor involved with the Greenwich Village artistic community, and started a studio in her own home when major museums such as the Metropolitan Museum of Art declined her extensive collection. The collection relocated to this gray granite building in 1966. The museum's most famous event is the Whitney Biennial, started by Gertrude Vanderbilt Whitney in 1932 to expose artists that couldn't exhibit elsewhere. The biennial showcases the trends of contemporary art, ranging from traditional media like painting and sculpture, to video, computer programs, live performances, and furniture. Among the 8,500 works the museum now holds are paintings, sculptures, and installations by Alexander Calder, Edward Hopper, Georgia O'Keefe, and Jasper Johns.

One of the lesser-known permanent installations in the Whitney is Charles Simonds' "Little People." Starting in the 1970s, Simmons hid 300 clay sculptures of an imagined diminutive civilization around the city, mostly in broken segments of dilapidated buildings and other hidden public spots. Of the very few that remain, three are visible from the Whitney if you know where to look. To see the sculpture *Dwellings*, stand in the stairwell eight steps up from the second floor and look inside the windowpane. Now look out the window at the building on the northwest corner of 74th Street. The second installment is on the right side of the building, underneath the smokestack of an exhaust, while the third is in a nearby window ledge.

Hotel Carlyle

Hotel Carlyle was named after Scottish writer and political theorist Thomas Carlyle, upon the recommendation of the daughter of hotel owner Moses Ginsburg. Most of Carlyle's essays were socialist and even fascist in character, which is funny considering that each guest room in the hotel has a direct line to Sotheby's auction house for private bidding. Since the hotel's opening in 1930, Presidents Truman, Kennedy, Johnson, Nixon, Carter, and Reagan have all stayed here, and during the Kennedy administration, the "Kennedy Duplex" was always kept vacant for the president's visits. At one point Jacqueline Onassis lived in a suite here as well.

The downstairs bar is named for Ludwig Bemelmans, the artist and children's author of the *Madeline* series. Bemelmans moved to New York from Austria as a rebellious teenager in 1914, after his parents forced him to choose between reform school and immigrating to the United States. He served in World War I and became a US citizen, and married his wife Madeleine in 1935. Although he named his series after his wife, many of his books were based on his daughter Barbara. Bemelmans painted fantastical Central Park murals on the walls of the hotel bar in exchange for a year and a half of accommodations for himself and his family. These paintings, restored in 2002, are his only surviving public murals.

The Solomon R. Guggenheim Museum

When the Guggenheim Museum first opened in 1939, it was called the Museum of Non-Objective Painting. Mineral mining tycoon Solomon R.

Guggenheim started the nonprofit art foundation, and early artists included Wassily Kandinsky, Paul Klee, and Piet Mondrian. Today the exhibits focus on modern and postmodern art, but range from motorcycles to Giorgio Armani suits. Guggenheim collections have opened around the world in Venice, Spain, Berlin, and Las Vegas. The museum board disputes the foundation's international expansion, some arguing that the new branches further the tradition of design innovation and creativity started by the original Guggenheim, others claiming that the expansion detracts from the New York archetype.

The unusual structure is architect Frank Lloyd Wright's only building in Manhattan, which he described as a "temple of spirit." Commissioned in 1943, the building took sixteen years to complete and was only finished after Wright's death in 1959. The construction is a concrete spiral hand-plastered over a steel frame that is narrowest at the base and widest at the top. The glass dome known as the Great Rotunda caps the structure and allows natural light to shine throughout. An interior ramp runs along the spiral, allowing visitors to see the entire collection in one long stroll, starting from the peak and making their way down. At first so controversial that its shape was likened to a toilet bowl, the Guggenheim building has become a New York landmark, even overshadowing the artwork inside.

COOPER-HEWITT NATIONAL DESIGN MUSEUM

This magnificent house served as steel tycoon Andrew Carnegie's 64-room mansion from 1902 until his death in 1919. During its construction, the neighborhood was considered déclassé, being so far uptown and so close to the "El" train, but after

Carnegie and his family moved here, other wealthy New Yorkers followed suit. The house introduced such technological innovations as a steel frame, central heating, and a passenger elevator. A three-story organ played wake-up tunes every morning at seven o'clock, and guests such as Mark Twain and Mme. Eve Curie were asked to autograph the dining room table cloth, to have their signatures later embroidered.

The Carnegie Corporation donated the property to the Smithsonian Institution in 1972, and the space became the Cooper-Hewitt National Design Museum, Smithsonian Institution by 1976. Amy, Eleanor, and Sarah Hewitt had founded the Cooper-Hewitt museum in 1897, in keeping with their grandfather Peter Cooper's vision for educational and research facilities for art and science, as exemplified by his all-scholarship university, Cooper Union, located in the East Village. The Cooper-Hewitt museum remains the only one in the country dedicated exclusively to design, with applied arts and industrial design, drawings and prints, textiles, and wall-coverings departments, as well as a comprehensive reference library and archive.

Carl Schurz Park

This waterfront park overlooks the Revolutionary War–era shipping passage known as "Hell Gate" for its strong currents. At the time, the area was filled with commercial ships that opted to navigate the faster ocean route into New York Harbor rather than the calmer waters of the Long Island Sound. The US Army cleared the nautical obstacles with a series of large explosions, and in 1910, after the city purchased the property from a private family, it was renamed for German immigrant Carl Schurz.

Schurz was a Union Army general in the Civil War and took an active role in American politics, even becoming the first German senator, representing Missouri. He also served on the Committee on Foreign

Affairs and as secretary of the interior under President Rutherford B. Hayes. In the 1880s, Schurz was editor in chief of the *New York Evening Post*, and in the 1890s he was an editorial writer for *Harper's Weekly*. He was a bold and aggressive writer, which gained him both fierce supporters and irate critics. He advocated that Germans maintain a deep connection with their heritage, a belief he combined with an open-minded patriotism toward the United States. The park that bears his name is appropriately located in Yorkville, the easternmost neighborhood on the Upper East Side, dominated by German and Hungarian immigrants throughout the twentieth century.

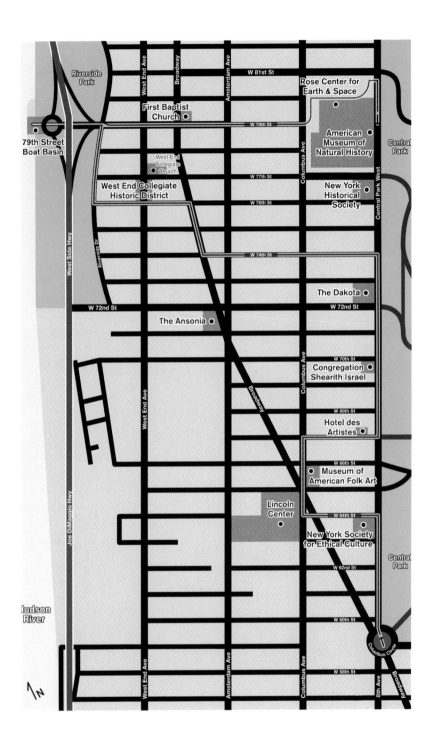

Upper West Side

*A*n ongoing rivalry exists between Upper East and Upper West Siders, the likes of which you might find at neighboring high schools. While both neighborhoods contain some of the most extravagant buildings in the city and parallel views of Central Park, residents of the Upper West Side tend to be thought of as more intellectual and creative than their corporate and political East Side counterparts. It is not surprising then, that Upper West Side celebrities include director Steven Spielberg, musician Paul Simon, and comedian Jerry Seinfeld.

Since its boom from 1885 to 1910, when some of the most ambitious buildings in the country were built in this area, artists such as painter Norman Rockwell, and writers such as J.D. Salinger and Herman Wouk have incorporated their experiences as Upper West Siders into their work. The establishment of Columbia University at the neighborhood's northernmost boundary in the 1890s and the creation of Lincoln Center in the 1960s only further defined the neighborhood as an intellectual and cultural epicenter. Even just glancing into the charming brownstones that line the side streets, you're likely to see more books, cultural artifacts, and artwork than the walls can hold.

The Upper West Side Walk

Start:	Columbus Circle, 59th Street and Central Park South
Finish:	80th Street and Central Park West
Length:	2 miles
Time:	2.5 hours

Refreshments: Fairway Café for fresh market food in a casual setting, Boat Basin Café for outdoor dining in the summer, Zen Palate for vegetarians, Isabella's for Mediterranean-inspired seasonal fare in a pretty setting, H&H bagels for the best bagels in New York at any hour of the day.

Sights: Columbus Circle, New York Society for Ethical Culture, Lincoln Center, Hotel des Artistes, Central Park West, the First Church of Christ the Scientist, Congregation Shearith Israel, the Majestic, the Dakota, the San Remo, the Ansonia, Beacon Theater, West End–Collegiate Historic District, Riverside Park, Hamilton Fountain, Boat Basin Café, Rose Center for Earth and Space, the American Museum of Natural History.

At Columbus Circle, look for the huge structure with the gold statuary on top. This is the Maine Monument, commemorating the explosion of the US battleship *Maine* in 1898. William Randolph Hearst, who ran the *New York Morning Journal*, decided to construct this monument to the disaster the very same week it occurred. The Spanish-American War started the same year the monument was completed, in 1913, in no small part because Hearst's newspaper depicted the explosion as an attack by the Spanish, even though it was more likely an accident. The bronze statues on top of the monument are cast from the guns of the *Maine*, and the little boy in front of the monument is a statue of Joseph Hearst, William Randolph Hearst's son. The Time Warner Center stands directly across the street, now a glorified shopping mall and media headquarters, but once the famous Majestic Theater where *The Wizard of Oz* premiered in 1903. In the middle of the circle is a tall column with anchors hanging off the sides and a large figure of Christopher Columbus on top. There are two monuments to Columbus in the city because two ethnic groups claim him as their own. The Italian version of the explorer sits in Columbus Circle, while the Spanish version resides on the literary walk in Central Park. Both were dedicated on the 400th anniversary of Columbus's voyage in 1842. Columbus Circle can be disorienting because it is a rotary in the generally straightforward grid of Manhattan; align yourself so that the Trump International Hotel and Tower is on your left, and walk north.

The building on the corner of 63rd and Central Park West has been home to the **New York Society for Ethical Culture** since 1911. Turn left on 64th Street and you'll see the main entrance, which was intentionally built on the side of the building for the sake of modesty. Walk straight on 64th Street until you arrive at **Lincoln Center**, the magnificent entrance of which you'll see by the time you get to Broadway. This performing arts complex houses the Metropolitan Opera in the building with the elongated arched windows straight ahead of you, the New York City Opera and New York City Ballet in the building to your left, and the New York Philharmonic in Avery Fisher Hall to your right. The Juilliard School is further right. A hidden art gallery called the Cork Gallery sits in the lower lobby of Avery Fisher Hall, free of charge, featuring work by lesser-known artists.

Upon exiting Lincoln Center, walk up the west side of the street so that Juilliard's Alice Tully Hall is immediately to your left. At 67th Street, turn right, and walk down the block between Columbus and Central Park West. 35 West 67th Street on your left, which is now the Makor/Steinhardt Center of the 92nd Street Y, used to be the Swiss Benevolent Society, established in 1883 to house New Yorkers of Swiss extraction, but most of the residents ended up being German, and English became the society's official language. Notice the ornamentation around the entrance of the Atelier, #33, and the real Tiffany glass lamp above the entrance of the Sixty Seventh Street Studio, #27. Across the street you'll see the ABC building. Many of the buildings on this block were built as artist studios, with double-height windows for light and to accommodate large canvasses, such as the **Hotel des Artistes**, with the flags above its canopy, which was built expressly for artists. The building on the south side of 67th Street, across the street from the park, is a great example of a studio building, as you can see by the size of its windows and the height of its ceilings.

Turn left, where you'll stumble onto the lobby of 75 Central Park West around the corner, which features old photographs of buildings in the neighborhood. Central Park West is lined with massive buildings that take up the entire block. Cross the street toward the park for a better view. The First Church of Christ the Scientist is on the corner of 68th Street and Central Park West. Though the Upper East and Upper West Sides both have an abundance of churches, socially mainstream churches like St. Patrick's Cathedral tend to be on the East Side, while unconventional churches like the First Church of Christ the Scientist, which was started by a group of women, tend to be on the West Side.

On the corner of 70th and Central Park West is Congregation Shearith Israel. Meaning "Remnant of Israel," this is the oldest Jewish congregation in the country, founded in 1654 by Portuguese Jews seeking refuge from the Spanish Inquisition. The congregation has grown throughout changing times, serving as a Continental ally during the American Revolution, when its rabbi, Gershom M. Seixas, corresponded with George Washington. This was the only synagogue in the city until 1825, when B'nai Jeshurun was formed, and many others followed.

The Majestic at 115 Central Park West was one of many large-scale apartment houses built before the Depression. Its architecture exemplifies German expressionism, evident by an emphasis on the horizontal juxtaposed with an emphasis on the vertical. The building was the home to mob bosses Meyer Lansky, Lucky Luciano, and Frank Costello, who was shot and wounded in the lobby in 1957.

The castle-like building across the street is the **Dakota**, built by Henry J. Hardenbergh, the same architect who built the Plaza Hotel, and next to it are the twin towers of the San Remo, each of which is topped by a 22-foot copper lantern. Residents of the San Remo have been recognized as giving more money to the Democratic Party than residents of any other building in the country. Make a left on 74th Street and notice how each brownstone on this street is more enchanting than the last. The owner of the Dakota built these row houses for those on the building's waiting list. A handful of these townhouses are now elementary schools located conveniently next to the park.

Continue another block toward Broadway, where you'll see the **Ansonia** directly across the street. Diagonally across from the Ansonia is the Beacon Theater, now used as a concert venue, but originally built as a movie theater by Samuel "Roxy" Rothafel, who built both the Roxy Theater and Radio City Music Hall. Continue to 76th Street and note the unusual architecture of the building on 77th and Broadway. The French-inspired Belleclaire, completed in 1903, embodies the popular art nouveau architecture of its time, which was sweeping Europe but ridiculed in the States. This landmark demonstrates that the boldest, most offensive designs of the time are often the ones that are later salvaged.

Turn left on 76th Street and walk toward West End Avenue. Take a moment to glance at the stunning row houses between 76th and 77th Streets on West

End Avenue, known as West End–Collegiate Historic District. At the end of 76th Street is Riverside Drive, overlooking Riverside Park. On the far side of the park, the West Side Highway borders the Hudson River. Hamilton Fountain, named for the real estate mogul Robert Ray Hamilton, a descendant of Alexander Hamilton, features a beakless eagle with its wings spread over a trough that fed water to horses at the time of the fountain's dedication in 1906.

Continue north on Riverside Drive to 79th Street. At the northwest corner of 79th, enter Riverside Park and walk through the underpass to your left. Stay on the path until you see signs for the Boat Basin Café. Follow the signs and descend the steps. You'll come to a café overlooking the Hudson River, where several houseboats are permanently parked. Retrace your steps to get back on 79th Street and walk one block east to West End Avenue. The church two blocks south is West End Collegiate Church, so named because the ministers were encouraged to be colleagues, not competitors. The neighboring all-boys' Collegiate School moved here in 1887, making it the oldest private school in the city. Continue on 79th Street until you reach Broadway, where you'll see eighteenth-century heir Charles Ward Apthorp's old mansion on the corner. Continuing east, you'll come to the First Baptist Church, the towers of which were intentionally left uneven. Some say this was intended to symbolize Christ's glory and the wait for his return; others argue that it symbolizes life as a work in progress.

Walk east on 79th Street past the Lucerne on Amsterdam, whose façade was the only part of the landmark preserved. At Columbus Avenue, you'll come to a dead end at Theodore Roosevelt Park. Walk into the park, past Alfred Nobel's monument, and ascend the stairs on the side of the brick building to the Arthur Ross Terrace of the American Museum of Natural History. The glass diorama containing planets and humans is the Rose Center for Earth and Space.

Exit the terrace through one of the gates prominently marked "Do Not Enter," walk down the stairs, and follow the path that brings you past the Rose Center's main entrance until you get back onto Central Park West. Your last stop, midway down the block to your right, is the neighborhood landmark the **American Museum of Natural History**, but local history buffs may prefer the New York Historical Society across 77th Street.

NEW YORK SOCIETY FOR ETHICAL CULTURE

Rabbi Felix Adler of Reformed Temple Emanu-El founded the New York Society of Ethical Culture in 1877 in order to inspire ethical activism and generate social reform. The society immediately established a visiting nurse service and a free kindergarten for working-class children, which became a lower and upper private school by 1928. The organization has addressed numerous social issues of its time, including housing discrimination, reproductive rights, and homelessness. As a religion, Ethical Culture preaches the value of human life and the interdependent relationship of individuals and their community. Its humanistic aims include an abolition of the death penalty, DNA testing to exonerate wrongfully accused prisoners, provisions for homeless women, and continued open dialogue on all topics.

HOTEL DES ARTISTES

This building, which opened in 1918, has served as a home to such famous artists as Norman Rockwell, Isadora Duncan, Rudolph Valentino, and Noel Coward. None of the apartments were built with kitchens because residents were expected to order all of their meals from the restaurant downstairs. If you peek inside the windows of the restaurant, you'll see paintings on the walls by Howard Chandler Christy, a resident artist who was famous for his paintings of pinup girls in the 1920s. He was a judge of the first

Miss America pageant and married the winner, whose naked body adorns these walls.

LINCOLN CENTER

Parks Commissioner Robert Moses developed Lincoln Center as part of his urban renewal program in the 1960s. The area spans seventeen blocks and is New York's premiere center for performing arts. At the time of its completion, the center was the first consortium of cultural institutions in a single location in the country. The community was so supportive of the project that 82 percent of the $185 million that went into creating Lincoln Center came from donations, while only 18 percent was derived from tax dollars. Lincoln Center gets its name from Lincoln's Inn Fields in London, which at twelve acres is not only the largest square in London, but historically also one of its most fashionable.

The bright Roman Travertine stone that comprises Lincoln Center is the same dazzling granite used in Rome, everywhere from the Trevi Fountain to the Vatican. Like the landmarks in Rome, the building's exteriors have been bleached white by the sun while the interiors remain a few shades darker.

There are seventeen buildings in the complex, including the New York State Theater, the Metropolitan Opera House, the Vivian Beaumont Theater & Mitzi E. Newhouse Theater, the Walter Reade Theater, the Julliard School, and Avery Fisher Hall.

THE NEW YORK STATE THEATER

The New York State Theater, which opened in 1964, is the home of the New York City Ballet and the New York City Opera. The aesthetic theme is that of a jewel box, evident by the chandelier lighting, the gold lattice of its inside railing, and the elevator walls that resemble a gold watchband. The creation of this theater marked the first time in history a theater was designed exclusively for ballet; the curved seating ensures that every seat in the house has an unobstructed view. When the opera performs, seating becomes more expensive with each ascending level because of the acoustics; however, when the ballet performs, seating becomes less expensive with each ascending level because of the visuals. The first balcony level is considered the most desirable place to take in either company's performances.

The Metropolitan Opera House

With 3,800 seats, the Metropolitan Opera House is the largest opera house in the world. It was built for the Metropolitan Opera, which has been performing since 1883. The colossal theater stands 43 stories high on its end, and two-thirds of the house is behind the stage. Of all the operas performed here, *Aida* and *La Bohème* are the most popular, and both are performed annually.

During the season, performers will tell you that the opera world becomes real and the real world becomes fake, but not everything is what it seems; the food on stage is rarely real, convincing though it might look, while the improvised conversation between the extras or "supers" on stage is almost always real. Many of the supers return season after season, so their time on stage is a great opportunity to catch up with each other.

The floating concrete staircase at the entrance to the theater was constructed by shipbuilders brought in from Maine, and has been graced by such aficionadas as Princess Diana of Wales and Jacqueline Kennedy Onassis, who used to take her daughter Caroline here when she was a child. Marc Chagall crafted the paintings that hang behind the arched windows, and the government of Austria presented the chandeliers to the opera house as a gift for the United States' help in World War II.

The Juilliard School

Juilliard was established in 1905 with the goal of creating a music academy in the United States that would rival the European conservatories. Dance and drama divisions have been added over the years, and famous alumni include Kelsey Grammar, Itzhak Perlman, Miles Davis, Laura Linney, Kevin Spacey, Yo-Yo Ma, Nina Simone, Val Kilmer (who was the youngest actor ever accepted at the school), and Robin Williams and Christopher Reeve, who were roommates and close friends. Robin Williams's acting teacher asked him to leave during his junior year to pursue a career as a stand-up comic, because the school didn't know where to place him. Juilliard later presented Mr. Williams with an honorary degree.

AVERY FISHER HALL

This was the first building of the complex to open, in 1962, designed by Max Abramovitz, who also designed the CIA Headquarters and the United Nations. The 2,700-seat theater sits directly above a subway in one of the most chaotic areas of the city, but it is completely soundproof. The acoustical advantage of wooden floors and walls and plaster ceilings enables the New York Philharmonic to play without any electronic assistance.

Leonard Bernstein, former conductor of the philharmonic, composed the music for *West Side Story*, which originally featured a storyline about a Jewish girl and Italian boy on the Upper West Side before neighborhood tensions changed in the 1960s and Puerto Rican and Italian families started clashing. The film was shot on the streets in front of the old, condemned buildings that were transformed into Lincoln Center. With the creation of the Lincoln Center arts complex, 700 of the families that were living on these streets were displaced. The neighborhood was promised 4,000 apartments by the center's completion, but only 400 were delivered.

THE DAKOTA

Completed in 1886, the Dakota marks the first time in New York that wealthy people shared a building with other wealthy people. It was a tenement in the true sense of the term, where three or more families shared the same address. Only the first seven stories were residences, while the top two floors were servants' quarters, housing a staff of 150. Supposedly the building got its name because it's so far north it may as well be in the Dakotas, but in reality, by the time the Dakota was built much of the real estate in the vicinity

was already bought up, including the plot for the American Museum of Natural History. Additionally, by the 1880s an elevated train connected the Upper West Side to the rest of the city, making it an accessible and desirable neighborhood to live in.

In fact, the Dakota was most likely named by its builder, Edward Clark, who proposed naming the West Side avenues after America's newest territories, such as Montana, Wyoming, Arizona, and Idaho, but only managed to name this building after the Dakotas. This was preferable to the nickname "Clark's Folly" that the Dakota received in its early stages of development when the project looked like it was going to be a financial failure. Not only did the Dakota end up being a financial success, with all of its apartments rented by opening day, but it also succeeded in its goal of revolutionizing urban dwelling by making collective living fashionable for the upper class.

The architect Henry J. Hardenbergh designed the structure to look like a fortress, and internally the building was created to resemble four vertical townhouses with an elevator in each corner. The apartments are arranged around a large private courtyard, which provides the units with light and air on all sides. When the building was declared a landmark, the one tenant that resisted was actress Lauren Bacall because she didn't want exterior air conditioners. She lost the landmark battle but got central air conditioning, as you can see by her apartment on the ground floor of the east side of the building (the only one without air-conditioning boxes).

The Dakota has long served as a residence for famous New Yorkers, and Rosemary Clooney, Madonna, Leonard Bernstein, Judy Garland, and Judy Holliday all lived here at various times. *Rosemary's Baby* was filmed and set on the top story of the building. Of course, the most well-known resident is John Lennon, who was shot and killed while entering the front door in 1980. On that December day, like most, John and Yoko signed albums as they left the building, including that of the perpetrator, Mark David Chapman. When they returned home, Chapman, who had been lingering in the cold for four hours, yelled "Hey John!" and shot Lennon four times. Instead of fleeing the crime, the murderer leaned against the building flipping through *The Catcher in the Rye*, waiting for the police to arrive. The book happens to be set in the same neighborhood. After Lennon's death, Yoko Ono chose to stay in the building, where she continues to live to this day on the fourth floor. She re-landscaped and donated the area of Central Park across the street known as Strawberry Fields as a tribute to her late husband.

The Ansonia

The Ansonia was built between 1899 and 1904 to be New York's largest and most palatial apartment hotel. Intended as a home for musicians, it took five years to build because of its fireproof structure, the pool in the basement, and the three-foot-thick soundproof walls that allowed residents to create music or even shoot guns (as in one rumored case) without disturbing their neighbors.

The building's unusual asymmetrical floor plan is due to its location on the slanted avenue of Broadway. There are indented light courts on all four sides of the building and the interior corridors form an "H." The building got its name from the family business of the developer: the Ansonia Brass & Copper Company.

Among its many famous residents, a number of New York Yankees have lived here, including Babe Ruth. The Broadway Producer Florenz Ziegfeld, best known for the *Ziegfeld Follies*, lived here in a thirteen-room apartment with his wife, actress Anna Held. Ziegfeld kept the exact same apartment one flight up for his mistress, Lilliane Lorraine, and when Anna found out about this setup fifteen years into their marriage, she summarily divorced him.

In the 1970s, the Ansonia was the home of the Continental Baths. This bathhouse, in the basement of the building, was the most swinging gay bathhouse in the city, and the venue where Bette Midler and Barry Manilow got their start with their hit stage show *Bathhouse Betty*. By the 1980s, the bathhouse subculture had become so mainstream that even the department store Bloomingdale's was selling Continental towels, and the basement turned into a famous sex club called Plato's Retreat. With the AIDS crisis in the 1980s, all bathhouses in the city closed down, and the once raucous underground level is now a Gristedes grocery store.

American Museum of Natural History

Inspired by Theodore Roosevelt's explorer's spirit, the museum features a dedication to the former president on its façade, adorned by statues of Daniel Boone, John James Audubon, and Lewis and Clark, while a grand monument of Roosevelt riding a horse stands in front of the building. Inside this preeminent science and research institution are 32 permanent exhibits and ever-changing current exhibits, covering everything from biology to geology, astronomy, ecology, and anthropology. Among the museum's most celebrated features is its 94-foot-long blue whale, which hangs from the ceiling of the two-story Hall of Ocean Life; the dinosaur halls; the rainforest display; the halls of minerals and gems housing the 563-carat Star of India sapphire; the Haida Canoe carved from the trunk of a single cedar; and of course, the numerous dioramas featuring all species of animals in their natural habitats.

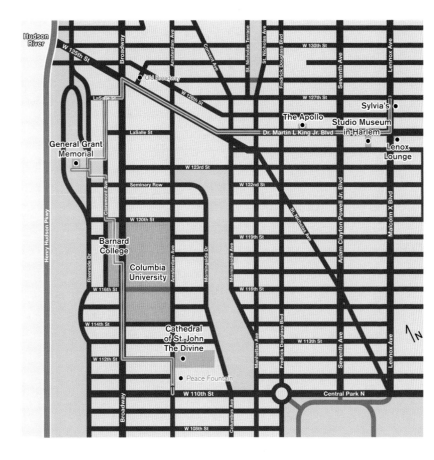

Upper Manhattan

*M*orningside Heights was once known as Asylum Hill for the lunatic asylum that stood here throughout the nineteenth century. Today Columbia University and Barnard College occupy the neighborhood, and the only craziness in the streets is that of the late-night bar scene typical of college towns. By the time the students wind down, Harlem church-goers start pouring into the Sunday gospel services a few blocks east. However, Upper Manhattan was not always so vibrant. This land was originally farmland, and in the 1870s Harlem's elevated trains and rapidly growing population led to the development of schools, churches, and cultural centers. As public transportation improved, real-estate speculators bought up every available lot in the vicinity, which led to overbuilding and extensive vacancies. By the early 1900s, landlords were forced to reduce rents to attract tenants, but still found a shortage in housing demand. Real-estate opportunist Philip Payton saw a fit between low-priced housing and a middle-class population that was denied access to other New York neighborhoods, and his firm effectively created an African-American community, which by the 1920s become the black cultural Mecca of the country. In this era, known as the "Harlem Renaissance," music, art, and literature flourished, and today Harlem remains the only predominantly black neighborhood in Manhattan.

Start:	Amsterdam Avenue and 110th Street
Finish:	Lenox Avenue between 126th and 127th Street
Length:	2.25 miles
Time:	2 hours

Refreshments: Bistro Ten 18 for elegant American cuisine in a cozy setting, Caffe Pertutti for Italian dining and outdoor seating, or Sylvia's for traditional soul-food favorites.

Sights: Peace Fountain, Cathedral Church of Saint John the Divine, Columbia University, Barnard College, Sakura Park, Grant's Tomb, Old Broadway, the Apollo, Studio Museum in Harlem, Lenox Lounge, Sylvia's

Note: Harlem is not always safe after dark, so if you stick around to enjoy its nightlife, be aware of your surroundings.

On 110th and Amsterdam Avenue, you'll arrive at the grounds of the **Cathedral Church of St. John the Divine**. Walking up Amsterdam, you'll pass sculptor Greg Wyatt's **Peace Fountain**, surrounded by the Children's Sculpture Garden. As you approach the cathedral, you'll see a dome rising so high that the Statue of Liberty could stand inside without touching her torch to the ceiling, which is adorned by Rafael Guastavino's artwork. Notice, as you approach the building, how its side reflects two very different architectural styles: the western side is Gothic and the eastern side is Romanesque. This is because architect Ralph Adams Cram took over after the original Heinz and LaFarge architectural duo ran into financial hardship, and he preferred a Gothic style to the team's initial Romanesque vision. When you first walk into the cathedral, pass through the dark wooden wall in front of you and look back to see that these are actually fifteenth-century German monastic pews. Directly in front of the pews is the "Peace Altar," installed by

Japanese-American woodworker George Nakashima in 1986. Nakashima hoped to make an altar of peace for every continent in the world from the same wood of an enormous black walnut log. Currently there are peace altars in Moscow, Russia, and Auroville, India. Although the artist died in 1990, the Nakashima Foundation for Peace continues to scout locations for these symbols of global harmony. The ribbons hanging above the altar symbolize all of the races of the world. As you continue into the church, note the granite and bronze medallions on the floor leading into the central nave; these are known as the Pilgrim's Pavement. The images represent the events in the life of Christ, and before the time of postcards and gift shops, visitors would make rubbings of these medallions to remind them of their experiences. There are seven bays on either side of the cathedral, dedicated to all aspects of civilization, including athletics, law, art, education, the environment, labor, poetry, and so on. Each bay features stained-glass windows depicting relevant biblical and contemporary scenes, such as the legal bay, which shows both Moses with his tablets and the signing of the American constitution. For a comprehensive explanation of the bays, pick up a *Treasures of the Nave* brochure at the front of the cathedral. Above the main entrance to the cathedral is the Rose Window. This window is so large that the Jesus figure cloaked in red in the center of the circle is actually 5' 7". The circumference of the window is meticulously measured to be 124 feet, the exact height of the Cathedral from the ground to the vaulting. Many of the building's measurements add up to 7 (1+2+4=7) because of the sanctity of this number in Christianity, evident in the Book of Revelations, the days of creation, and the deadly sins. A biblical garden sits next door to the church to its rear, containing all of the plants from the Bible.

Exiting the cathedral, follow 112th Street west to Broadway. On the corner of 112th and Broadway you'll see Tom's Restaurant, the exterior of which appears as the diner in *Seinfeld* episodes. Turn right up Broadway and you'll see Kim's Video and Music on your right, with a subversive selection of music, movies, and books. Across the street is the popular college bar, the West End. On 114th Street, you'll come to Alfred Lerner Hall of Columbia University, the campus's student life center, followed by the college bookstore and the main gates of **Columbia University** on 116th Street. King George II of England founded the university in 1754, naming it King's College. The school was renamed Columbia College in 1784, and later became a full academic and research institution. Among the research conducted here was the "Manhattan Project," in which university physicists produced the atomic bomb. Wander around the campus and, as you exit the main gates, continue up Broadway. You'll pass by the Miller Theatre on your right, where various speakers, student theater groups, and international musicians perform year round.

Cross 117th Street to get to **Barnard College**, and walk through the front doors, turning left to get to the LeFrak Gymnasium. A plaque next to the door reads "In commemoration of the last public speech of Malcolm X given on February 18, 1965, in this gymnasium." If you get a chance to peek into the room, you'll see that it is flooded with light from large arched windows on three sides. Walk all the way to the north side of the hallway and exit through the side door, past Wollman Library and Altchul Auditorium, through the doors of the picturesque Millbank Hall. You'll notice that the exterior of the building is far prettier than the interior, and as you descend either staircase, exit through the double set of doors straight ahead (ignore the emergency exit sign).

Turn left outside of the building and make a right onto Claremont Avenue. The Riverside Church on your left is a grand structure modeled after a thirteenth-century Gothic cathedral in Chartres,

France. The church prides their congregation on "The Three I's," as an interdenominational, interracial, and international spiritual institution. Union Theological Seminary on your right aims to combine theological education with an urban environment to allow ministers to respond to the needs of the city.

On 122nd Street, you'll see the Manhattan School of Music and the Jewish Theological Seminary. It is no surprise that West 122nd Street is known as Seminary Row. Turn left and walk up the steps to Sakura Park. Sakura means "cherry blossom" in Japanese, and in the spring the cherry blossoms here are magnificent. Continuing west, you'll get to General Grant Memorial or **"Grant's Tomb,"** the largest mausoleum in the United States. Ascend the steps and walk inside, taking in the exhibit of Grant's life as a citizen, general, and statesman. Don't forget to look up at the magnificent domed ceiling and down at the crypt, which contains the coffins of Grant and his wife surrounded by bronze busts of Grant's top generals. Exit right and follow the mosaic walls and benches inspired by Antonio Gaudi's architecture in Barcelona until you return to the front of the memorial.

When you get back onto Riverside Drive, turn left, and you'll see Riverside Park bordering the Hudson River. Cross at the first light up Riverside Drive back toward Sakura Park and follow the angled road down, past International House. At Tiemann Place turn right, and at the subway lines on Broadway turn left. Cross Broadway at 125th Street, heading east. You'll see a sign for Old Broadway in the middle of the block. The oldest road in the city, Broadway— or Bloomingdale Road as it was known in colonial times—continued in this direction. Today the large road under the subway lines is known as Broadway, while this small street is referred to as Old Broadway. The Old Broadway Synagogue can be found up the block, a relic of the early-nineteenth-century Eastern European Jewish community that resided here.

When you come to Roosevelt Triangle, which divides 125th Street, veer left heading toward the Apollo. The **Apollo Theater** needs no introduction, as it is the city's third most popular tourist destination. The once-segregated theater has since become a landmark of black entertainment and popular culture. If you continue east on 125th Street, you'll come to the Studio Museum in Harlem on the next block. This museum showcases current and past artists of African descent. The museum store also has a nice selection of posters, publications, and souvenirs. Since 1939, Lenox Lounge, on the southeast corner of Lenox

Avenue and 125th Street, has served the likes of musicians Billie Holiday, John Coltrane, and Miles Davis. The Jazz Club in back, known as the Zebra Room, was a frequent hangout of writer James Baldwin and Malcolm X.

Turn left onto Lenox Avenue and walk two blocks to Sylvia's. This family-run soul-food restaurant is a neighborhood institution, and its menu items include traditional southern food like fried chicken, barbecue ribs, and collard greens. Not only is it an inviting place for a meal, but the photographs on the wall also display some of the restaurant's better-known patrons, such as former President Bill Clinton, who works down the block.

PEACE FOUNTAIN

As its bronze plaque states, the fountain represents the triumph of good over evil. Archangel Michael embraces a giraffe, symbolizing peace, in his right hand, while decapitating a devil with his left hand. Additionally, a large smiling sun faces east, while a tired moon faces west. The base of the sculpture takes the shape of a swirling double helix as a nod to the

first DNA images discovered in the early 1980s when the sculpture was conceived. Greg Wyatt is a Columbia alumnus and his work can be seen throughout the university's campus.

CATHEDRAL CHURCH OF ST. JOHN THE DIVINE

This massive church is the largest Gothic cathedral in the world. In the Middle Ages cathedrals were the only public buildings in the community, and the church strives to keep this tradition alive with a full schedule of community events. Cathedral School next door used to be a choir school, but now it is a private elementary and middle school where live peacocks roam, three of which are colored and two of which are white. The church also has an artists-in-residence

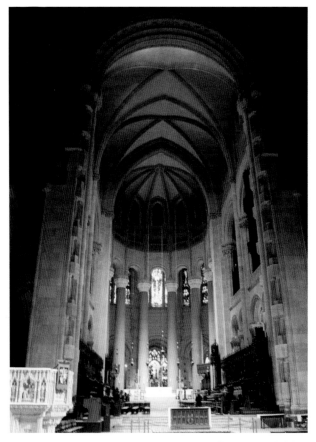

program, for artists like Greg Wyatt (see above). The chairs in the cathedral are all movable to maximize the space's flexibility. The events that take place here range from philharmonic concerts to the Blessing of the Animal in October, where worshippers stand wall to wall with their pets, and everything from a camel to a bowl of algae is marched down the aisle. Look for Duke Ellington's white piano, donated by his family after his memorial service was held here.

COLUMBIA UNIVERSITY

Walk through the main gates, down the tiled path to the center intersection of the campus, where you'll see the Butler Library on your right and the Low Library on your left, both designed by the architectural firm

of McKim, Mead and White in the 1890s. The bronze *Alma Mater* figure sits on the steps of the Low Library with an open bible in her lap and lamps symbolizing wisdom and teaching on the arms of her chair. The sculptor, Daniel Chester French, created this figure in 1903, but is best known for the Lincoln Memorial in Washington, DC. You'll see two fountains at the base of the library steps. Ascend the steps on the east side and walk straight toward the Charles H. Revlon Plaza, named for the late founder of the Revlon cosmetics company. The large stone creature on top of Columbia Law School's Greene Hall is Jacques Lipschitz's *Bellerophon Taming Pegasus*. In Greek mythology, the mortal Bellerophon tries to fly the winged horse Pegasus to the heavens, only to be thrown by the king of gods, Zeus.

Circle the sculpture garden, which affords a view down the length of Amsterdam Avenue on either side, and upon exiting, turn right toward a cast of Auguste Rodin's *Thinker*, appropriately placed in front of the philosophy building.

Walk back toward Low Library, turning right before you get to the steps, onto the brick path leading to the university chapel. St. Paul's Chapel is inscribed with the Latin phrase *Pro Ecclesia Dei*, meaning "church of god." If possible, enter the chapel (the side door is usually unlocked) and stroll through the inside.

Exiting the chapel, follow the same brick path north and turn left at Avery Hall, walking past Uris Hall of Columbia Business School, the front of which displays Australian artist Clement Meadmore's 1968 steel sculpture, *Curl*. Continuing forward, you'll see the

Scholar's Lion sculpted by 1971 Columbia alumnus Greg Wyatt, who also designed the Peace Fountain near St. John the Divine. Get back to the main gates by turning left and walking down the library steps.

BARNARD COLLEGE

In 1889 Barnard was the only women's college in New York City, but Barnard has always had a partnership with Columbia University academically and socially, with joint clubs and extracurricular groups. The campus itself has been well preserved, and four of Barnard's campus buildings—Milbank, Brooks, Hewitt, and Barnard Halls—are on the National Register of Historic Places. Among the college's famous alumnae are novelist Erica Jong, *Sex and the City* actress Cynthia Nixon, Pulitzer Prize–winning journalist Anna Quindlen, *Movin' Out* choreographer Twyla Tharp, and singer Suzanne Vega, who wrote the song "Tom's Diner" about the *Seinfeld* diner on 112th Street. Writer Zora Neale Hurston was the school's first African-American graduate in 1927.

Grant's Tomb

By the time of his death in 1885, Civil War general Ulysses S. Grant was considered a hero by both the Union North, for which he fought, and the Confederate South. The eighteenth president was not only victorious in every aspect of the Civil War, but also a gracious winner once the war was over. He was firm in his protection of the equality of former slaves, while immediately trying to restore peace in the South and reunify the country. Perhaps this is why 90,000 people donated a total of over $600,000 to complete the twelve-year construction of his tomb. On the day of his funeral, one million New Yorkers turned out to pay their respects, and buildings all over the city were

reverently draped in black. All three branches of government marched in the procession, including then President Grover Cleveland and his cabinet, the entire Supreme Court and almost every member of Congress. The tomb was dedicated on April 27, 1897, on what would have been Grant's 75th birthday. His wife, Julia, was laid at his side in an identical sarcophagus upon her death in 1902.

THE APOLLO

Perhaps the most conspicuous Harlem landmark, the Apollo Theater is known throughout the country for its rowdy shows, in which celebrities and novices alike get a chance to perform while the crowd gets a chance to voice their opinions on said performances. Amateur night, which has been televised since 1987, has propelled the careers of legendary stars like Ella Fitzgerald and the Jackson Five, while ending the careers of countless others. Once onstage, Apollo hopefuls rub the trunk of the Tree of Hope, which once stood on a Harlem street where performers lined up daily to be selected for gigs.

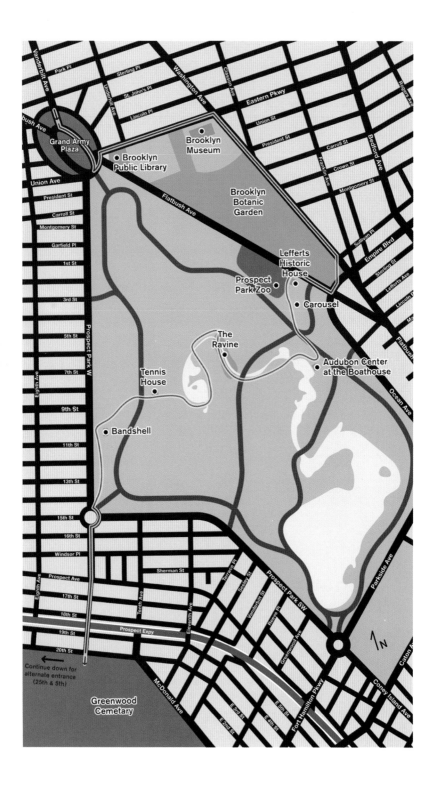

Brooklyn

In 1855 Brooklyn was the third-largest city in the United States, following Manhattan and Philadelphia. At the time, half of Brooklyn's population was foreign-born, many of whom were Irish escaping the potato famine. The immigrant tradition continues to this day, and with ever-increasing rents in Manhattan as well as a limited housing supply, Brooklyn has become an economically viable alternative for many New Yorkers. Populated by young creative types as well as the kind of small boutiques and live music venues that have been displaced from Manhattan, the borough is also a vibrant shopping and nightlife destination.

Prospect Park is to Brooklyn what Central Park is to Manhattan. The park was designed in 1866 by the same architectural team of Frederick Law Olmsted and Calvert Vaux, who initially wanted to connect the two parks with a series of wide boulevards, and since it was constructed after Central Park it is considered the duo's masterpiece. In this later project the team was uncompromising in their creation of a truly rural retreat, and although many structures and sculptures were erected subsequent to the park's completion, the space maintains a naturalistic feel that lures Brooklyn-ites to its rambling grasses year round.

The Brooklyn Walk

Transportation:	Take the 2 or 3 train to Grand Army Plaza
Start:	Grand Army Plaza
Finish:	Greenwood Cemetery
Length:	2.5 miles
Time:	2 hours

Refreshments: Terrace Café for outdoor dining in warmer months, Windsor Café for omelets, Elora's for Mexican, or Two Little Red Hens for dessert.

Sights: Grand Army Plaza, Prospect Park, Brooklyn Public Library, Brooklyn Museum, Brooklyn Botanical Gardens, Prospect Park carousel, Lefferts Homestead, Prospect Park Zoo, Audubon Center, Lullwater Pond, Binnen Bridge, Nethermead, the Ravine, Esdale Bridge, Bandshell, Harmony Playground, Greenwood Cemetery.

Note: For a shorter walk, stop at the exit of Prospect Park; for a longer walk continue along Prospect Park West to Greenwood Cemetery.

Start at Grand Army Plaza, the grand entrance to **Prospect Park**, both of which were designed by Central Park architects Calvert Vaux and Frederick Law Olmsted. At the Bailey Fountain, which was the park's first feature in 1867, follow the granite Belgian blocks toward the Soldiers' and Sailors' Memorial Arch of 1892, which honors the Union military of the Civil War. This dramatic park structure resembles the Arc de Triomphe in Paris, and was intended to give Prospect Park the splendor of Europe's cosmopolitan plazas. As you walk through the arch, you'll see bronze cavalry figures and massive war scenes depicted in sculpture on the other side. On Saturdays, the plaza is the site of the second largest farmers' market in New York City after the Union Square market in Manhattan.

Be careful crossing Eastern Parkway, the city's first parkway, and walk to the last column with an eagle on it on your left as you face the park's entrance. You'll see a columned shelter for a trolley line that closed in the 1950s. The Egyptian-styled building to your immediate left across Flatbush Avenue is the Brooklyn Public Library, constructed in 1941 with the help of millionaire Andrew Carnegie. Cross over to the library and follow Eastern Parkway around the side of the building. You'll see the Children's Library behind the main building and steps that lead to Mount Prospect Park, a smaller park nearby.

At the top of the steps, follow the path to your right, and turn left so that you're walking between the large field and the playground. Walk back toward the street and you'll come to a classically designed building housing the **Brooklyn Museum**. Turn right at Washington. To your left are the Brooklyn Heights and Clara Barton High Schools, and to your right is the Brooklyn Botanical Gardens. There is an entrance fee for the gardens, so if you would like to look around, exit at Flatbush Avenue and make your way toward the Prospect Park carousel. Otherwise, follow the garden's gate down Washington Avenue past the historic Administrative Building and Palm House on your right, and past the railroad tracks to Empire Boulevard. Turn right at Empire and cross Flatbush Avenue back toward Prospect Park.

Walking away from Empire Avenue, enter the park on the walkway by the second stone column, which will bring you to the carousel. $1 carousel rides are available Thursdays through Sundays during park hours. Turn right at the carousel and you'll see a white house on your right known as Lefferts Homestead. One of few surviving Dutch Colonial farmhouses in Brooklyn, this house was home to the Dutch Leffert family from its construction in 1777 for at least four generations. The period rooms are preserved with the original architecture and furnishings from the 1820s.

The Prospect Park Zoo is on your left, offering glimpses at 80 species of animals, including the Asiatic horned frog, cotton-topped tamarin, emerald tree boa, Hamadryas baboon, four-horned sheep, porcupine, wallaby, and red panda. Make your way back to the carousel and follow the path marked as leading to the Audubon Center. At the Lullwater Pond, on which you can go on an electric boat ride in warmer months, you'll see the Audubon Center at the boathouse to your left. The center was the nation's first wildlife preservation facility and also serves as the park's visitor center.

Make a right and cross the Binnen Bridge. You'll see the Music Pagoda on your right, which hosts events for theatrical and community organizations. Follow signs to the Ravine, passing a brook on your right and the grassy Nethermead on your left. Pass through the Nethermead Arches and turn right into the Ravine, following the path around. The rugged terrain of the Ravine, designed to evoke the scenery of the Adirondacks, cuts through the most remote and topographically diverse region of the park.

Exiting the Ravine, turn left and cross the Esdale Bridge. Take your first right and stay right, following signs to Longmeadow. Take the middle path through Longmeadow, past the Tennis House on your right. Built in 1910 as a shelter for lawn tennis players, the Greek temple–like structure provides environmental education programs to the public and hosts an art gallery. Feel free to walk over for a better view.

Stay on the Longmeadow path across West Drive and walk toward the Bandshell on your left. One of the most popular park attractions, this 2,000-seat plaza holds concerts, films, and performing arts events. Roam through Harmony Playground and exit by the bronze climbing sculpture of a long-haired nymph. Continue on the walking path closest to the street heading away from the playground, and exit the park by the Pavilion movie theater by Bartel-Pritchard Circle. Named for World War I soldiers Emil Bartel and William Pritchard, the circle is flanked by two large columns topped with copper lanterns, designed by preeminent New York architect Harry Thaw.

To get to **Greenwood Cemetery** by foot, walk a half-mile west on Prospect Park West. Note that on a weekday you'll have to walk another half-mile from the side of the cemetery to its main entrance. If you're feeling up for it, upon exiting Prospect Park, cross Prospect Park Southwest and make a left at the Oak Park Pharmacy onto Prospect Park West. You'll pass Farrell's Bar & Grill, a 1933 remnant of the once Irish Park Slope neighborhood, as well as the Roman Catholic Holy Name of Jesus School and Church on Windsor Place, which dates back to 1878. At 20th Street, you'll come to a side entrance of Greenwood Cemetery. If this entrance is closed, turn right on 20th Street and follow the gate all the way down to the main entrance on 25th Street and Fifth Avenue. When you come to the main entrance, be sure to pass through the Victorian Gothic gate, designed by Richard Upjohn, who also designed the Trinity Church at Wall Street in Manhattan. If the sales office is open, pick up a map of the cemetery to navigate the more interesting monuments. Be sure to look for the small 1911 chapel near the main entrance. Also, the Civil War Memorial at the top of Battle Hill at the intersection of Battle Path and Liberty Path is particularly noteworthy for its zinc sculptures. It is the highest point in Brooklyn and the site of the Battle of Long Island in the Revolutionary War. Nearby, a Revolutionary War statue in the form of the goddess Athena waves to Lady Liberty across the water.

Prospect Park

Long before it was developed as a public space, the area that comprises Prospect Park was the setting for the Battle of Brooklyn, one of the major clashes of the Revolutionary War. In the summer of 1776, the Continental Army fought to deflect an attack from the south of the park, and although the Americans lost the

battle, the army managed to stave off British troops long enough to allow General Washington's forces to escape to New Jersey. Much of the layout of the park still resembles its 1776 form, thanks to designers Olmsted and Vaux, who re-landscaped the land while preserving its integrity. In its planning stage, Prospect Park was meant to serve a similar purpose as Central Park, providing an escape for locals, as well as a reason for wealthy residents to relocate to the city. The result is a neighborhood respite that feels larger and less structured than it is, best taken in through hours of aimless wandering.

Brooklyn Museum

Opened in 1897, the Brooklyn Museum is the second-largest art museum in New York City, after the Metropolitan Museum of Art. Like the Met, the museum is a classically designed, massive Beaux Arts building, conceived by the design firm of McKim, Mead and White, who also constructed Grand Army Plaza and the old Pennsylvania Station in Manhattan.

Daniel Chester French, who sculpted the Lincoln Memorial in Washington, DC created the two allegorical figures known as *Brooklyn* and *Manhattan* that adorn the museum's exterior. In 2004 the museum's deteriorating 28-foot staircase was replaced by a glass, grass, and steel semicircular stoop meant to effectively scoop visitors inside. Besides their varying current exhibits, the third floor contains the finest collection of Egyptian art outside of Egypt, and the fifth floor boasts a comprehensive collection of Auguste Rodin sculptures.

GREENWOOD CEMETERY

At the time of its founding in 1838, it was said that a successful New Yorker would enjoy life on Fifth Avenue and death in Greenwood. Perhaps this is why, by the 1850s, Greenwood Cemetery was the second biggest tourist attraction after Niagara Falls. Considered the most prestigious cemetery in New York, the still operational burial ground holds 600,000 graves, among them some of the most illustrious figures in New York history. Composer Leonard Bernstein is buried here, as well as wealthy manufacturer Peter Cooper, abolitionist preacher Henry Ward Beecher, *New York Tribune* founder Horace Greeley, telegraph inventor Samuel F.B. Morse, stained glass artist Louis Comfort Tiffany, and notorious Tammany Hall leader William Marcy "Boss" Tweed.

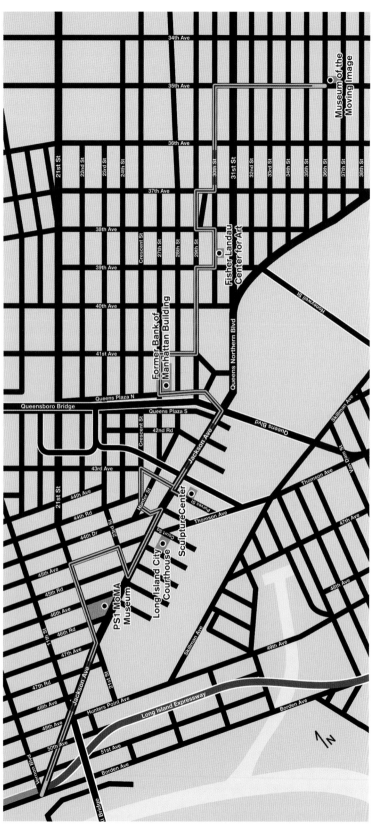

LONG ISLAND CITY, QUEENS

Queens

The most striking aspect of Queens is how much more of the sky you see here than in Manhattan. A hybrid of urban and suburban life, Queens offers shorter buildings, wider streets, and lower rents than Manhattan, which explains why a contemporary art community has flourished in Long Island City. The largest borough geographically, Queens has also become the most ethnically diverse county in the United States, and it is here that you'll find some of the most authentic multinational cuisine in the country, reflecting the area's Russian, Korean, Greek, Latin, Caribbean, Italian, Portuguese, and Lebanese populations, to name a few.

Queens celebrities have long drawn from their experiences growing up in this borough, ranging from songwriters Paul Simon and Art Garfunkel, to fashion designer Donna Karan, film director Martin Scorsese, and real-estate developer turned game show host Donald Trump. Additionally, much of East Coast hip-hop is rooted in Queens, and Nas, 50 Cent, Ja Rule, LL Cool J, Mobb Deep, and Run-DMC all started out in this part of town. In recent times Long Island City has flourished with innovative galleries and prestigious museums, and strolling through the neighborhood to catch the art indoors and on the street is surely the most interesting way to take it all in.

Transportation:	Take the 7 train to the Vernon Blvd/ Jackson Ave Station
Start:	50th Avenue and Vernon Boulevard
Finish:	35th Street and 35th Avenue
Length:	1.75 miles
Time:	1.5 hours

Refreshments: Brooks Restaurant founded in 1892, if you want to try one of the city's oldest restaurants; Napoli Pizza and Pasta for Italian; S'Agapo for Greek.

Sights: P.S. 1 MoMA, Hunters Point, Citicorp Tower, McKenna Triangle, New York State Supreme Court Building, Sundial, SculptureCenter, Queens Plaza, Bank of Manhattan Building, Fisher Landau Center for Art, Kaufman Astoria Studios, American Museum of the Moving Image.

Note: Neighborhoods in Queens vary in safety from block to block, so be aware of your surroundings and if possible, bring a friend.

You'll exit the train on 50th Avenue and Vernon Boulevard. Cross Vernon Blvd to the squat, red brick Café Henri and continue down 50th Street. Look at the row houses to your left and brickwork to your right. As you walk, note the juxtaposition between the old and new buildings, which is characteristic of Queens. Glancing behind you you'll see the Empire State Building. Turn left onto Jackson Avenue and you'll see the Citicorp Tower straight ahead of you.

Turn left onto 21st Street and you'll see a US post office on your left. The massive brick **P.S. 1 MoMA** contemporary art museum is on your right. The main entrance is on Jackson Avenue. Follow 21st Street past 45th Road until you get to 45th Avenue and make a right. The 1880s Italianette row houses date to back when this area was an independent municipality. Today the street is called Hunters Point.

Cross 23rd Street and walk back toward Jackson Ave. You'll come to the Citicorp Tower and the McKenna Triangle directly across the street from it. This small plot of land honors local World War I hero Major James A. McKenna. The 60-foot flagpole is actually the mast of a ship.

Turn left at the Citicorp Tower and notice the exquisite New York State Supreme Court Building courthouse across Jackson Avenue to your right. Built in 1876 before Queens' 1898 consolidation with New York, the building was almost destroyed by a fire in 1904 and then rebuilt by 1908, which is why the structure incorporates French and neoclassical architectural elements. Staying on Jackson Avenue, cross 44th Drive, then make a left onto Crescent Street and another left onto Hunter Street. The sundial on the island in front of you honors Long Island City heroes.

Turn right, back onto Hunter, and make another right to 43rd Street, making your way back to Jackson Avenue. Cross Jackson Avenue and walk down Purves Street, where you'll see the SculptureCenter on your left. Located in an old trolley repair shop, the organization has held exhibitions for emerging artists in a number of locations since 1928. This most recent incarnation of the facility dates to 2001 and was designed by Maya Lin, architect of the Vietnam Veterans' Memorial in Washington, DC.

Back on Jackson Avenue, make a right and follow it all the way down to the tangled maze of subway rails that is Queens Plaza. Cross Queens Boulevard and Queens Plaza to your left, and follow the curve along Queens Plaza North. The large brown building with the four-faced clock on top is the former Bank of Manhattan Building. Walk toward the building, and follow 41st Avenue away from the subways to the red brick building with white trim on 29th Street and 41st Avenue, known as Brewster Newcomers High School. Follow 29th Street to 39th Avenue, and on your right you'll pass the First Reformed Church of Long Island

City, now the Korean Philippo Presbyterian Church. On your left, you'll pass the Roman Catholic St. Patrick Church.

Turn right on 39th Avenue and left on 30th Street and you'll come to the **Fisher Landau Center for Art**, the interior of which is entirely white. Turn left on 38th Avenue and cross 29th Street. Notice the slanted Old Ridge Road that is inconsistent with the rest of the roads in Queens. Turn right on 37th Avenue and you'll see vibrant graffiti covering the building on your right.

Turn left on 30th Street and stay on 30th until 35th Avenue, at which point turn right and walk to 35th Street. You'll come to Kaufman Astoria Studios, and behind it the **American Museum of the Moving Image**, which will be of particular interest to movie buffs and aspiring filmmakers. To get back to a subway, after exiting the museum turn left on 35th Avenue, walk two blocks to Steinway Street and make a left. You'll see a subway station on 34th Avenue running G, R, and V lines.

P.S. 1 MoMA

Public School 1 was built in the 1880s, at a time when the population of Long Island City numbered 48,000, and schools, churches, municipal buildings, and residences were filling the streets. When the school closed in 1963, students and teachers matriculated at three other schools in the area. The building was used as a municipal warehouse until 1975, when the city-funded Institute of Art and Resources coalition transformed the space into one of the more experimental art museums in New York City. P.S. 1 MoMA started off as a nonprofit arts center dedicated to transforming abandoned buildings into exhibition and performance spaces, and the museum continues to focus on contemporary art and emerging artists.

FISHER LANDAU CENTER FOR ART

Emily Fisher Landau is a wealthy art collector who ran out of room in her homes to hang her art, so she hired Max Gordon, architect of advertising magnate Charles Saatchi's London gallery, to build this futuristic museum in a former parachute harness factory. Since 1991, this facility has freely exhibited works of art from the 1960s to the present, and today the collection tops 1,000 pieces. Artists include Andy Warhol, Barbara Krueger, Cy Twombly, Chuck Close, Ed Ruscha, Robert Rauschenberg, and Willem de Kooning, all of whom Emily Landau has known personally, having purchased works of art directly from their studios. A portrait of Fisher Landau by Andy Warhol even hangs in the entrance of the exhibition space. Landau refers to the museum as her "living room": it is the one place where she can finally contemplate her beloved acquisitions collectively. Happily, the rest of us are invited to do the same.

AMERICAN MUSEUM OF THE MOVING IMAGE

The Astoria Studio was once the largest production facility in the United States outside of Hollywood. From the time of its inception in the 1920s, the studio served as Paramount's East Coast production facility, focusing on independent film production throughout the 1930s. The facility served as the US Army's Photographic Center from World War II until the 1970s, at which point the nonprofit Astoria Motion Picture and Television Center Foundation was formed. By 1982, ownership of the site was transferred to the city of New York and the organization set about creating a museum that would maintain a comprehensive collection of motion picture and television archives, as well as educate the public with exhibitions, lectures, and screenings. The result was the extensive American Museum of the Moving Image.

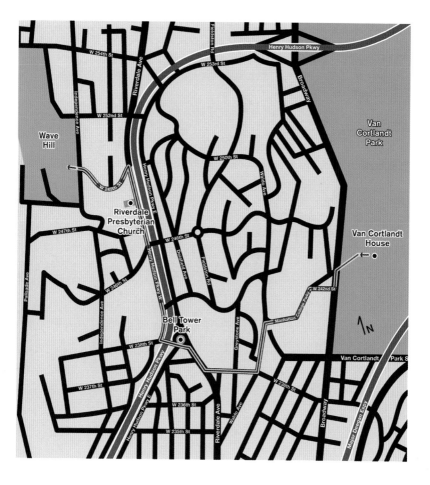

The Bronx

The Bronx is the only New York City borough that is part of mainland North America. Almost a quarter of the region is parkland, and over the years the open spaces have provided homes for many New York icons, such as Yankee Stadium, the Bronx Zoo, and the New York Botanical Garden, as well as Pelham Bay Park and Van Cortlandt Park, the largest parks in the city. The borough is also the hometown of music icons Mary J. Blige, Grandmaster Flash, Jennifer Lopez, Carly Simon, and Billy Joel, writers E.L. Doctorow, Don DeLillo, and Edgar Allen Poe, as well as Stanley Kubrick, Regis Philbin, and Ralph Lauren.

One of the lesser-traveled parts of the Bronx is Wave Hill, a riverside garden acquired by conservationist George Walbridge Perkins in 1903. After its purchase, Perkins immediately set about renovating the grounds to enhance the property's astounding views, and he is largely responsible for the Wave Hill's internationally acclaimed landscaping. Situated on the Hudson River, the property has served as a secluded getaway to various political and intellectual notables, such as Theodore Roosevelt, Mark Twain, and author William Makepeace Thackeray, and since 1960, the grounds have provided the Bronx with a public garden and cultural center.

The eighteenth-century **Van Cortlandt House** is the oldest house in the Bronx. The design is unusual because of its solid square shape and keystones in the south windows. The caretaker's cottage and colonial revival herb garden that sit beside it were added in 1917. In front of the main house you'll see a statue of Civil War hero Major General Josiah Porter in full dress uniform. He climbed the ranks of the 22nd Regiment of the National Guard of New York, which commissioned sculptor William Clarke Noble to construct the bronze figure in his honor.

Walk back out to Broadway and cross the street so that the park is to your left. You'll come to a Burger King. Turn right here and left on Manhattan College Parkway. Stay to the right so that you're on 242nd Street. Then turn left at Waldo Street, and right on 238th Street. You'll be walking uphill. Cross Riverdale

Avenue and turn right, crossing 238th and 239th Streets. Now cross Henry Hudson Parkway East so that Bell Tower Park is to your right. The 500-ton tower and Spanish bell were cast in 1762 for a Mexican monastery. US General Winfield Scott captured them in 1847 during the Mexican War. On Hanukah, this small park features

the largest menorah in the Bronx.

Turn right on Henry Hudson Parkway West and stay left on the sidewalk so that the houses are to your immediate left. You'll pass the Riverdale Presbyterian Church on your left, designed by the same architect as St. Patrick's Cathedral in Midtown Manhattan. The 1863 church was part of a movement toward country living as a means of escaping the tumultuous atmosphere of the city during the Civil War. The rocky cliffs across the street are reminiscent of Manhattan's geology before Governor DeWitt Clinton leveled the entire island to establish the 1811 grid.

Turn left on 249th Street and follow it down to **Wave Hill** at the end of the road. The grandiose private homes on either side of 249th Street give you a sense of the affluent suburb of Riverdale. President John F. Kennedy lived here from 1927 to 1931 while attending the prestigious Riverdale Country School right around the corner from Wave Hill. The easiest way to leave the Bronx via public transportation is walk back on 249th Street toward the Henry Hudson Parkway and make a right. The 7 or 10 bus leads to the 1 or 9 train station.

Van Cortlandt House

The land on which Van Cortlandt House is built was once the hunting grounds of the Mohican Indians; at the time a large marsh sat directly to the south. Dutch settlers took over the area in 1646, and colonial merchant Jacobus Van Cortlandt purchased the land in 1694. He was mayor of New York intermittently between 1710 and 1720. Jacobus's son Frederick built this house in 1748, and it remains the earliest preserved in this borough. During the American Revolution, the house served as headquarters for George Washington and other British and American military commanders. Washington kept campfires burning on this ground to deceive the British while crossing the Hudson River, and Frederick Van Cortlandt's son Augustus hid the city records from the British in a family vault nearby. Van Cortlandt House has been operated as a museum since 1896, and the city bought and converted the surrounding land for use as a park in 1899.

Wave Hill

Jurist William Lewis Morris built his country house on the site of present-day Wave Hill in 1843, and sold it to a wealthy publisher by the name of William Henry Appleton in 1866. During Appleton's residence, his houseguests included British biologist Thomas Henry Huxley and evolutionist Charles Darwin, as well as Teddy Roosevelt, who stayed with him in the summers of 1870 and 1871. American writer Mark Twain leased the house from 1901 to 1903, and commented one winter, "I believe we have the noblest roaring blasts here I have ever known on land; they sing their hoarse song through the big tree-tops with a splendid energy that thrills me and stirs me and uplifts me and makes me want to live always." J.P. Morgan partner George W. Perkins eventually purchased the property, which was later filled by such illustrious guests as Italian conductor Arturo Toscanini, who lived here in the 1940s, and chief members of the British delegation to the United Nations, who stayed here in the 1950s, including the Queen Mother Elizabeth. The Perkins family deeded the property to the public in 1960, and it has provided a serene recluse for Bronx residents ever since.

Staten Island Botanical Garden

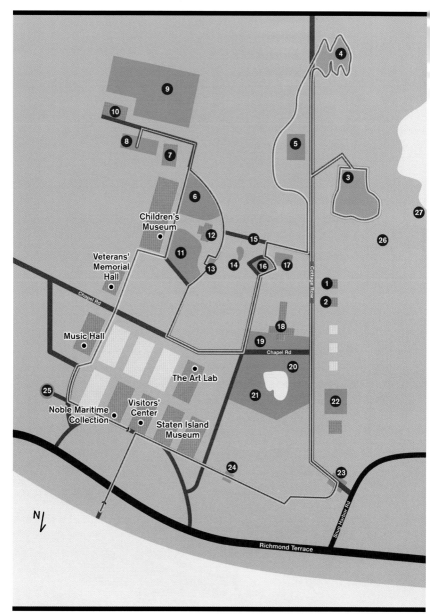

Key to Gardens

1. The New York Chinese Scholar's Garden Visitor's Center & Gift Shop
2. Café Botanica
3. The New York Chinese Scholar's Garden
4. Garden of Healing
5. Connie Gretz's Secret Garden
6. Lions' Sensory Garden
7. Anthony R. Gaeta Center For Horticulture & The Environment
8. Italian Garden
9. Vineyard
10. Barn & Farm
11. Shade Garden
12. WTC Educational Tribute
13. Butterfly Garden
14. Peony Collection
15. Allée
16. Herb Garden
17. White Garden
18. Carl Grillo Glass House
19. Perennial Garden
20. Pond Garden
21. Dogwood Collection
22. Rose Garden
23. Lynne Steinman Rhododendron Collection
24. Captain Randall Garden
25. Neptune Fountain Garden
26. Plantation
27. Wetlands

Staten Island

Staten Island is the most suburban, but fastest growing, borough of New York City. It is sometimes called "Staten Italy," because it has a larger percentage of Italian Americans than any other county in the US. Fittingly, Italian-born explorer Giovanni da Verrazano was the first to discover this area, sailing through the narrows between Staten Island and Long Island in 1524. Today the Verrazano-Narrows Bridge that bears his name provides road access from Staten Island to Brooklyn. Until its construction in 1966, the ferry was the only way to enter or leave Staten Island, and for most residents it remains the most efficient.

Snug Harbor Cultural Center lies in one of the island's more secluded areas. Founded by wealthy merchant Robert Richard Randall, who upon his death requested that his money fund a retirement home for seamen, Sailors' Snug Harbor offered housing, dining, entertainment, and medical facilities to the sailors that retired here, at one point numbering 1,000. By the 1970s, the retirement home was no longer of use and relocated to North Carolina, where the organization continues to operate. The grounds of the Staten Island home were converted to an arts village in 1976, with the establishment of the Snug Harbor Cultural Center.

your left. Modeled after Sissinghurst Castle garden in Kent, England, the garden consists entirely of white flowers and foliage that glow silver in the moonlight.

Walk down this road, known as Gazebo Road, where you'll see the only remnant of Snug Harbor's original four gazebos. These gazebos were installed to cover the airshafts that ventilate the underground tunnel system back when the harbor contained a hospital and tuberculosis center. Gazebo Road will lead you to Chapel Road, where you'll find the entrance to the Carl Grillo Glass House and Perennial Garden on your left, named for an avid Staten Island gardener. Every December, Snug Harbor arranges a Christmas tree lighting in front of the glass house.

Walking away from the greenhouse, you'll see the Art Lab on your left, which offers fine art classes, workshops, and exhibits. To your right are the studios where Art Lab artists produce their work, and to your left are dance studios and a preschool.

Turn right onto Melville Road and walk into the Butterfly Garden to your right, where budilia and butterfly weed are planted to lure visiting butterflies and migratory monarchs. To your left stands the 9/11 Tribute Center, devoted to Staten Islanders killed in the September 11 terrorist attacks. A large number of firefighters and police officers live on Staten Island, so the community was especially affected by this tragedy. Photos of nearly all of Staten Island's victims, numbering approximately 280, are on display at this center, which was formerly a morgue for deceased retirees. The Lions' Sensory Garden nearby features tactile and sensory-enhanced plants for the visually impaired. The path forks a few steps down. Veer right and follow the lampposts to the brick horticultural building at the far end. To your left you'll see the Italian Gardens. The original plan for Snug Harbor Cultural Center called for gardens from all over the world. The Italian garden is particularly appropriate considering that Italian-Americans constitute the largest ethnic demographic on Staten Island.

Retrace your steps and follow this path down to the Staten Island Children's Museum, the entrance to which is around the corner. Housed in a former barn, the museum features interactive galleries, workshops, and special performances.

Exiting the museum, stay left until you come to the large bell dedicated to World War II Merchant Marines. The bell stands in front of the Veterans' Memorial Hall Playhouse, a former chapel now used for performing arts events. Across the street is the Music Hall, the second oldest theater in New York City after Carnegie Hall. The venue opened as a gas-lit vaudeville hall showing silent movies to the retired seamen that lived here, and today Staten Island theater companies and music groups use the hall as a performance space.

Follow the path alongside the Music Hall to its classically designed façade. The building next door is the Great Hall, once used as a library and reading room. The hall also contained a game room that sailors nicknamed Monte Carlo. The space now serves as a banquet and reception hall for Snug Harbor events. The Neptune Fountain by the main road is named for the Roman god of the sea. Walk around the fountain and then head back to the buildings from which you started.

The second building on your left is the Noble Maritime Collection, a maritime museum and study center named for John A. Noble, a sailor turned lithographer whose houseboat studio is on permanent display here. The museum offers printmaking classes in his honor. From the visitors' center you can catch the bus back to the ferry or learn about other hidden Staten Island attractions at the information kiosk inside.

THE STATEN ISLAND FERRY

The 25-minute ride to Staten Island is scenic, frequent (running 24 hours), and free of charge. At one point there was a fare for the ferry, but the current law is "one city, one fare," so all public inter-borough transportation in New York City is the price of a single subway ride (except for the ferries, which are completely free). The ferry is a rare opportunity for New Yorkers to tune out and enjoy 25 minutes of unhurried transit, and even in inclement weather you'll see ferry riders standing on the outside platforms enjoying the ocean air. Apparently the ferry can also be a good venue for meeting new acquaintances, as the three men who founded the Staten Island Museum met on a ferry ride in 1876. The ride offers views of the Statue of Liberty and Lower Manhattan, as well as the Brooklyn, Manhattan, and Verrazano bridges.

WHITEHALL AND ST. GEORGE FERRY TERMINALS

The most recent versions of both the Staten Island and Manhattan ferry terminals were completed in 2004, and both terminals aim to make the commuting experience more pleasant. Whitehall Ferry Terminal in Manhattan has a veranda deck heated from below with rainwater, while the St. George Ferry Terminal in Staten Island has a green roof planted with flora that attracts monarch butterflies passing Staten Island on their way south. From the terrace above the green roof you can see "Postcards" across the water, a September 11 memorial created by artist Masayuki Sono, in the form of a white,

winged sculpture. On axis with the World Trade Center site, both sides of the sculpture's marble exterior are carved with images of Staten Islanders who were killed in the terrorist attacks.

New York Chinese Sculpture Garden

Snug Harbor is home to the Staten Island Botanical Garden, the most exotic of which is the Chinese Sculpture Garden, a one-acre adaptation of the Liu Yuan garden, or "garden for lingering," near Suzhou, China. Designed by distinguished Chinese landscape architect Gongwu Zou and completed in 1999, this Ming garden is the first authentic Suzhou classical garden in the United States. Its special features include Chinese courtyards, lotus ponds, and teahouses, as well as 2,500 tons of Tai Lake limestone imported from southern China, and carved wooden and ceramic calligraphy plaques. All of the labor was either done in China or by Chinese artisans temporarily relocated for the project, and much of it was done by hand in traditional classical style to ensure authenticity. The garden also includes Chinese vegetation and eighteenth- and nineteenth-century Chinese furniture.

Secret Parts of Town

There are certain parts of Manhattan that are not only off the grid, but also have a different energy than the rest of the city. These hidden nooks are devoid of the taxis, pedestrian traffic, and Zagat-rated restaurants that define many of the city's streets, and instead offer space and scenery for quiet contemplation. Often located in the vicinity of the most populated areas of the city, the secret parts of town tend to fall under the radar of most New Yorkers because there is no obvious reason to visit them. Yet all of these spots have an intangible appeal that will be of particular interest to natives looking for solace from the urban jungle and visitors seeking to get off the beaten track.

ROOSEVELT ISLAND

Start: Broome Street between Centre Street and Cleveland Place

Transportation: Take the N, R, W, 4, 5, or 6 to 59th Street/Lexington Avenue, or the F to 63rd Street/Lexington Avenue. Walk to 60th Street and east to Second Avenue.

Roosevelt Island is a two-mile-long island running parallel to Manhattan on the East River. For a tiny piece of land, its name and use have gone through several incarnations, starting with Mannahannock, Algonquin for "long island," when it was inhabited by Native Americans; to Varckens Eylandt or "hog island," when the Dutch purchased the land in 1637; to Perkens Island, named by the British in 1667, followed by Manning Island; and Blackwell Island by 1686. Elizabeth Blackwell of the Blackwell family was the first woman in the United States to receive an MD, in 1849. The City of New York purchased the island in 1828 for municipal use, and by 1921 the island was known as Welfare Island because of its prisons, poorhouses, hospitals, and asylums. The Blackwell Penitentiary, which imprisoned actress Mae West and Tammany Hall leader William Marcy "Boss" Tweed, closed in 1935, along with most of the other institutions, and by 1973 the island was renamed Roosevelt Island and built up with residential housing complexes. Today only a few historic landmarks remain, but the water views make the island a refreshing alternative to the density of the city, while the whole of the island is easily walkable from end to end.

A Stroll through Roosevelt Island:
Catch the tramway, which runs every quarter hour, on Second Avenue and 60th Street. The five-minute tram ride runs along the Queensboro, or 59th Street, Bridge (as in the Simon and Garfunkel song), and offers a good view of the east side of Manhattan and the water. Upon exiting the tram, walk toward the playing field and get on the pedestrian trail by the water. Turn left so that you're walking north. The pink bridge on your right is Queensbridge.

After you pass a playground, make a left and walk toward the gray 1796 Blackwell House. Make your way to the front of the house to see the porch where millionaire Peter Cooper negotiated the $32,000 purchase of the island for New York City in 1828.

Then walk up Main Street. You'll come to the Episcopal Chapel of the Good Shepherd, built in 1899 with its large bell outside that once summoned worshippers throughout the island. Keep walking past Tony Capobianco Field, toward a hammered metal walkway to your right that leads to the Octagon Park soccer field. Continuing along the path, you'll come to a private garden dead end. This community garden is composed of about 100 plots owned by island residents, the plants of which range from the large rose garden you can see from the fence to all varieties of flowers and vegetables. See if a friendly neighbor will open the gate to let you wander through.

At the fire station next to the park, turn left and continue north on the walking path by the water. To your left you'll see the Octagon, a domed tower built in 1839 that served as the island's lunatic asylum. When you reach the northernmost tip of the island, you'll come to a lighthouse that stands alone, surrounded by water. This lighthouse guided ships coming through the choppy part of the river known as Hell's Gate, where the East River turns sharply into the Harlem River. The structure is named after Vicky Holland, a beloved community member who died in 1979 at age 48. Walk around the lighthouse and start walking back toward the tram on the west side of the island. You'll come to Dayspring Episcopal Church on your left, a former Metropolitan Hospital chapel. To your right, the bow of a ship aimed at Manhattan's eastern skyline rises out of the ground. You'll also come to some playful copper sculptures in the water on your right, installed in 1996 by public artist Tom Otterness.

Continue past the tram and, if possible, walk through the gate at South Point and along the unpaved road to the ruins of the 1856 Smallpox Hospital. The gate is usually locked so be careful not to get locked out. The stone castle is striking and eerily serene, its large Gothic structure desolate but for ivy and shrubs. Head back to the tram and enjoy dangling through the sky while the sensation lasts.

SOUTH STREET SEAPORT

Transportation: Take the A, C, J, M, Z, 2, 3, 4, or 5 to Broadway-Nassau/Fulton Street Station and walk down Fulton Street to Pearl Street.

New York's harbor has historically been its greatest political, economic, and geographic strength, and throughout the nineteenth century the "Street of Ships" was one of the most important shipping hubs on the globe. At the time, the seaport community catered to all maritime needs, and the cobblestone streets were packed with ship chandleries, sail makers, and figurehead carvers, as well as pubs, restaurants, and brothels. Robert Fulton launched the world's first steamship in 1807 from South Street Seaport, and in 1816 Captain Charles H. Marshall founded the Black Ball Line, introducing the concept of regularly scheduled boat departures. Reliable transatlantic ship service revolutionized trade by allowing merchants to

count on both incoming and outgoing deliveries, making New York City the fastest and most efficient center of maritime activity. No longer an international port town, South Street Seaport is more understated these days, but the area nevertheless buzzes with street life and public performances, and offers a number of boat tours on the river.

A Stroll through South Street Seaport:
When you get to Pearl Street and Fulton, you'll see a lighthouse memorializing the victims of the 1912 *Titanic* tragedy. Pearl Street was Manhattan's original shoreline. The land east of Pearl did not exist in the 1600s when the Dutch owned the island, but by the 1700s, British law stated that if a landowner lived on the waterfront and filled the water with landfill, the land was his. So the shoreline grew to Water Street, then Front Street, and eventually to South Street. Each name represents the last barrier to the water and each street east of Pearl is made of landfill.

As you walk to South Street, you'll pass one of the earliest nineteenth-century commercial structures in the city on your right. The Schermerhorn Row Galleries now house art galleries, clothing stores, and the South Street Seaport Museum, and were the first buildings in the country to be lit by electricity. The original exterior has been well preserved. Feel free to walk through the cobblestone shopping area before crossing South Street over to the seaport.

As soon as you cross South Street, you'll see a visitors' center on your right. A large Pizzeria Uno stands at Pier 17 to your left. Directly across from Pier 17, next to the visitors' center, is the eye-catching four-masted 1911 *Peking*. The three-masted 1885 *Wavetree* sits beside it, and the small boats assembled between the two are early twentieth-century tugboats. The red boat in between the *Peking* and Pier 17 is the *Ambrose* lightship, a small 1908 boat that guided ships into port. All of these boats conduct regular tours.

Exiting the port, turn right on South Street so that you're walking uptown under the FDR Drive. The drive was constructed from World War II debris that was used to counterbalance the weight of US ships. You'll pass wholesale fish operators M. Slavin & Sons on your left and the old 1822 Fulton Fish Market on your right. Get on the pedestrian walkway by the water, where you'll see the Brooklyn and Manhattan bridges in front of you, and Peck Slip to your left, with a painted mural of the Brooklyn Bridge on its brick façade. In its heyday, Peck Slip was a center for port activity. Now the area is turning residential, due to the fish market's move to Brooklyn. The walkway extends several blocks north, so continue your stroll along the water, taking in the fresh sea air.

You'll see some of the most expensive townhouses in the city tucked away in this relatively quiet area by the East River, called Sutton Place. Effingham B. Sutton, a prospecting equipment shipper during the San Francisco Gold Rush, built the original brownstones here in 1875. Most of the low-rise, single-family homes have private gardens overlooking the water.

A Stroll through Sutton Place:
Walk to 57th Street, as close to the water as you can get, to see the stately townhouses built by the Vanderbilts and the Morgans in the 1920s. The H.J. Heinz family lives at 1 Sutton Place in the Vanderbilts' old home, and the current secretary-general of the United Nations lives at 3 Sutton Place, where J.P. Morgan's daughter lived. The architect of these homes intentionally opted for old bricks salvaged from tenement wrecks rather than new bricks, to give the houses an antiquated feel.

Walk up to 58th Street and out to the lookout point that offers an unobstructed view of the water and of Roosevelt Island across the way. Continue uptown, passing under the Queensboro Bridge and cross the FDR Drive entrance to get to 61st Street. Turn left past the Twenty-Four Sycamores Playground and cross Sutton Place to get to the 1826 Mt. Vernon Hotel and Museum in the middle of the block. New York's only surviving day hotel was built in 1799 as a country escape for New Yorkers living at the southern tip of the island. Today the house serves as a museum, with eight furnished period rooms and historically designed gardens.

BROOKLYN BRIDGE

Transportation: Take the J or M to Chambers Street, or the 4, 5, or 6 to Brooklyn Bridge/City Hall, or the R to City Hall. At the southeast corner of City Hall Park, follow signs to the Brooklyn Bridge.

When the Brooklyn Bridge was completed in 1883, it was the longest suspension bridge in the world and New York's tallest structure. Unprecedented in both size and technology, the bridge used steel wire instead of cast iron, and employed caissons, or large underwater chambers, to attach the stone towers to Manhattan's bedrock at the bottom of the East River. The project encountered a number of obstacles. The idea of a bridge itself was controversial because Manhattan and Brooklyn were two separate cities at the time, and Brooklynites feared becoming a suburb of Manhattan, which had twice its population, but the cities nevertheless consolidated in 1898. Also, due to the nature of the construction, many workers suffered from caisson disease, or "the bends" while working on the project. Workers returning to a low-pressure environment too quickly after descending to the high-pressure environment underwater often doubled over in pain and went into convulsions back on the surface. Over the course of construction, 200 workers suffered from this decompression sickness and 20 died from it. Washington Augustus Roebling, the bridge's chief engineer and son of the bridge's designer John Roebling, lost the use of his legs because of the bends, and depended on his wife, Emily Warren Roebling, to take over for him as supervisor.

The technological innovations learned throughout the engineering process were later taught to the rest of the world. Although many bridges today employ the Brooklyn Bridge's design, the public was dubious about its stability at the time of its construction. Within a week of the bridge's opening, on Memorial Day 1883, a pedestrian tripped and someone screamed thinking that the bridge was falling. The rumor spread quickly through the crowd and the panicked mob scrambled to get back on land, killing twelve in the stampede. A few months later, P.T. Barnum led a herd of 21 elephants across the bridge, declaring once they reached the other side that the bridge was safe for every kind of traffic.

A Stroll across the Brooklyn Bridge:
Enter the bridge by City Hall Park. As you approach the Manhattan tower, you'll see the Manhattan and Williamsburg Bridges on your left, as well as the Manhattan skyline. The white ventilation shaft tower of the Brooklyn-Battery Tunnel sits on Governor's Island to your right. Currently unoccupied, the island contains several Revolutionary-era houses. South Street Seaport and the Statue of Liberty are also on your right. You are standing 135 feet above the river, a height that guarantees neither death nor survival if jumped. Suicide

attempts, stunts, and bets have all had mixed results. A strategic jumper by the name of Clara McArthur bounded off the bridge in 1895 with 20 pounds of sand in her stockings in order to land feet first. She survived the fall, avoiding the internal injuries she would have sustained had she landed on her side.

At the Brooklyn tower, you'll see a plaque honoring John, Washington, and Emily Warren Roebling. As the head engineer of the bridge during the time of its completion, Emily Roebling was given the first ride across, with a rooster, symbolizing victory, on her lap. Toward the end of the bridge, descend the stairs to your left. Then follow the stone wall on your right to Cadman Plaza Park. Enter the park and at Middagh Street cross Crown Plaza and turn left on the other side. Walk through the red brick Whitman Owner Corp. Townhouses to get to Henry Street. These industrial structures replaced Walt Whitman's former home.

Walk with the traffic on Henry Street and turn right on Orange Street. Plymouth Church of the Pilgrims is on your right. In front of the church stands a statue of Henry Ward Beecher, an orator, leader of the abolitionist movement, and minister of the church in this neighborhood, known as Brooklyn Heights, the one-time center of abolitionism. His sister, Harriett Beecher Stowe, wrote *Uncle Tom's Cabin*. Turn left on Willow and wander around the well-preserved row houses in the area. Brooklyn Heights has more Civil War–era buildings than any other neighborhood in the five boroughs. Willow Street alone is rich in literary history. Truman Capote wrote *Breakfast at Tiffany's* and *In Cold Blood* in the basement of 70 Willow Street, and Arthur Miller wrote *The Crucible* at 155 Willow. On your right you'll see the waterfront Brooklyn Heights Promenade, a frequent movie setting and a quiet place to sit or stroll.

The green window-paned brick high-rises that comprise Peter Cooper Village and Stuyvesant Town cause the neighborhood to look more like a college campus than an upper-middle-class residential community. Nevertheless, this is a family-oriented part of town with fields, playgrounds, carnivals, sports teams, and clubs, but no dogs (they're not allowed). Peter Cooper Village is named for millionaire and Cooper Union founder Peter Cooper, who lived near this area, and Stuyvesant Town is named for the last Dutch governor of Colonial New Amsterdam, Peter Stuyvesant, who owned a country house on the land 200 years earlier. The residential development was constructed in 1945, and soon had the largest concentration of veterans in the country.

A Very Short Stroll through Peter Cooper Village and Stuyvesant Town:
On First Avenue and 21st Street, you'll see the entrance to Peter Cooper Village. Walk into the village, past the basketball court and the river playground, and cross the two-way street to your right known as 20th Street Loop. Walk through the "Do Not Enter" traffic signs to Stuyvesant Town. The Stuyvesant Oval is directly ahead of you and serves as the central landmark of the community.

Transportation:	Take the 5 to Bowling Green, or the 1 or 9 to South Ferry. Walk through Battery Park toward the Hudson River to get to the Ferry station.

On any given day one is struck by the number of languages spoken on the ferry ride to Ellis Island, but considering that this small piece of land was the processing point for the over 12 million immigrants that entered the United States between 1892 and 1954, it is appropriate that so many different nationalities are represented on the ferry rides alone.

Named for Samuel Ellis, who was the first private owner of the island in the 1770s, Ellis Island became the property of the US government in 1808. It was immediately used as part of New York harbor's defense system, just in time for the War of 1812. The island opened as a federally operated immigration station on January 1, 1892, but by the 1920s, immigration laws had become increasingly strict, and quotas limited the number and nationality of immigrants that were allowed into the country. These quotas prohibited the physically and mentally impaired and illiterate, and greatly restricted immigration from certain parts of the world, especially Asia. In 1924 no more than 150,000 immi-grants would be admitted per year, which stood in stark contrast to the 1.25 million immigrants that were processed in 1907 alone.

By the end of World War I, United States em-bassies around the world served as immigrant processing centers, and in 1965 Ellis Island became a national monument. Since its 1984 restoration, which was the largest of its kind in U.S. history, the museum has offered educational facilities, exhibitions, and an interactive experience to visitors seeking to learn about their heritage and the cultural evolution of the United States.

A Stroll through Ellis Island:

To get to the ferry, enter Battery Park and walk through the World War II Merchant Marine and Army Transport Monument, which takes the form of eight inscribed stone walls shielded by a large black eagle. The boat ride is about 50 minutes long. You may choose to explore Liberty Island before continuing on, but regardless of whether or not you disembark you'll have a nice close-up view of the Statue of Liberty. When you arrive at Ellis Island, you'll see the Ellis Island Immigration Museum directly in front of you, the only building on the island that is open to the public. The first room you enter, entitled the "Baggage Room," is where immigrants chose to either check their bags, possibly to never see them again, or to carry their belongings throughout the three- to five-hour immigration process. Also on the first floor, behind the museum's reproduction of immigrants' luggage and crates, is an exhibit called "The Peopling of America," which illustrates immigration trends in the United States and the world. The cafeteria, gift shop, theaters, and American Family Immigration History Center are on the ground floor as well.

The staircase to the right of the museum's entrance as you walk in is a replica of the 1924 staircase that assisted immigration officers in determining the physical condition of arriving passengers. As people made their way up the stairs, officers looked for symptoms such as shortness of breath or dizziness, indicating a medical condition. The inspection continued in the large room on the second floor, where officers were required to conduct "six-second physicals" in order to process the thousands of immigrants that were arriving daily. Doctors used different colored chalk to write symbols on immigrants' coats, such as "H" for heart problems, "P" for pregnancy, "S" for senility, and "X" for suspected mental illness. After the medical inspection was over, immigrants provided legal information in this room before moving on. The historical touches that linger include the original benches where immigrants waited to be processed, the desks where the immigration officers stood, and the tiled ceiling created by the Spanish Guastavino brothers in 1917, as well as the three Tiffany's lamps hanging from the ceiling, one of which is a reproduction (the one closest to the benches). The staircase with the red railing behind the officers' desks was designed to sort immigrants that had completed the immigration process into their future destinations. The right side of the stairs brought people to a railroad, the middle was for those who were being further detained, and the left side of the stairs led to a waiting room where immigrants reunited with family members and loved ones.

If you look out the grand windows on the Statue of Liberty side, you'll see the medical wards built in 1911 to accommodate immigrants with medical conditions. The windows on the opposite side offer a view of the downtown Manhattan skyline. The second floor also houses two exhibits, one of which is entitled "Through America's Gate," and which takes you through the Ellis Island arrival and inspection process, and the other "Peak Immigration Years," which takes you through the horrors and highlights of immigrant life in America between the years 1880 and 1924. Continuing to the third floor, you'll find an example of the dormitory rooms where immigrants were detained, as well as four more exhibitions and a library. Most of the exhibits on this floor center on Ellis Island itself, its evolution, expansion, and restoration.

On your way out of the museum, be sure to check out the remains of Fort Gibson near the American Immigrant Wall of Honor around the corner. Built in 1794 of sod and wood, and rebuilt in 1807 of brick and stone, Fort Gibson is one of the earliest forts constructed to protect New York's harbor. The portion that remains includes 25 percent of the original structure.

Transportation: Take the M4 bus to its last stop (about an hour from midtown), or take the A train to 190th Street. An elevator will take you to street level, where you'll see Fort Tryon Park.

This castle-like structure in northern Manhattan's Fort Tryon Park is a branch of the Metropolitan Museum of Art. Known as the Cloisters, the collection is dedicated to the art and architecture of medieval Europe, and includes sculpture, tapestries, manuscripts, stained glass, enamels, and ivories dating from 800 CE, most of which comes from the twelfth to fifteenth centuries. The building itself incorporates elements from five medieval French cloisters (Saint-Michel-de-Cuxa, Saint-Guilhem-le-D'sert, Bonnefont-en-Comminges, Trie-en-Bigorre, and Froville), and features landscaping consistent with medieval works of art and poetry. Medieval cloisters provided shelter between buildings within a monastery, and here the passageways serve a similar purpose, contributing to the flow of the museum's galleries. The initial collection evolved from that of American sculptor and medieval art collector George Grey Barnard, who started his own museum in the early 1900s. His collection was purchased by John D. Rockefeller in 1925 and has been a part of the Metropolitan Museum of Art ever since. Riverside Church architect Charles Collens designed the current building in 1938, and today the Cloisters offers lectures, gallery workshops, concerts, and family programs.

A Short Stroll through the Cloisters:
Much of the Cloisters' appeal is its secluded atmosphere, evoking the quiet pace of an earlier time.

For peaceful reflection, the gardens and terraces are just as much of a treat as the artwork itself. Masterpieces can be found in every room, such as the famous set of seven South Netherlandish tapestries depicting "The Hunt of the Unicorn," contributed by Rockefeller himself, featured in the aptly named Unicorn Tapestries Room, as well as the early-fifteenth-century French illuminated book of hours, *Les Belles Heures de Jean*, located in the Treasury. Starting at the visitors' entrance, work your way counterclockwise to view the collection chronologically.

CONSERVATORY GARDEN AND HARLEM MEER

Transportation: Take the 6 train to 103rd Street and walk west toward Central Park.

The Conservatory Garden is an overlooked part of Central Park because it is so far from the action of its larger grassy areas. Unlike the majority of the park, the garden is a designated quiet zone, and most visitors come alone or in pairs. The gardens are intentionally designed to evoke a European feel, with English, Italian, and French influences. There are a variety of flowers and plants in the meticulously maintained landscape, as well as fountains and small statuary, and plaques on the benches from the park's Adopt-a-Bench program are often inscribed with messages for loved ones.

The Harlem Meer is named for the Dutch word for lake, for its proximity to the former Dutch swampland of Harlem. This area of the park served as a series of fortifications for the Revolutionary War, when the British had the advantage of a lookout point, and the War of 1812, when the Americans benefited from the same lookout point. Military buffs might enjoy climbing up to the summit of Fort Clinton, located on a steep hill directly behind the Meer, to fully appreciate the strategic view.

A Stroll through Conservatory Garden and Harlem Meer: If you're taking the train, walk west on 103rd Street to Fifth Avenue, where you'll come to the New York Academy of Medicine, an institution that focuses on urban health and also has the world's largest cookbook collection, thanks to a doctor who equated good food with good health. You'll also see the Museum of the City of New York, featuring exhibits that highlight the city's evolution and diversity. Across the street, the James Marion Sims Monument commemorates the controversial nineteenth-century surgeon, famous for his many innovations in modern gynecology, but criticized for his treatment of black female slaves. Heading uptown, you'll pass El Museo del Barrio on 104th Street, a museum dedicated to Latino art, before coming to the massive gates of the Conservatory Garden on 105th Street. These 1894 gates once stood outside the home of wealthy shipping and railroad magnate Cornelius Vanderbilt (now the site of Bergdorf Goodman).

As you enter the garden, you'll see the Italian-style Central Garden directly in front of you and the Conservatory Garden fountain behind it. Turn left and walk down the path to the English mazelike shrubbery of the "Secret Garden." Frances Hodgson Burnett, English author of the 1909 book *The Secret Garden*, donated the fountain in the center of the garden to the children of the City of New York. Its bronze figures depict the book's central characters. At the far end of the garden toward Central Park, ascend the steps to the wrought iron gazebo, where medallions list the thirteen colonies that comprised the original United States. At the north end of the garden is a French circular hedge surrounding the Untermeyer Fountain, named for the family that presented it to the city in 1947. The fountain is also known as the Three Dancing Maidens. Just beyond the northern end of the gardens is the Harlem Meer. Populated by many varieties of geese, duck, and swans, as well as fish and turtle species, the Meer is one of the many artificial bodies of water in Central Park. As you follow its path, you'll come to a red brick building with a shingled roof known as the Charles A. Dana Discovery Center. The center offers information about the park, including maps and a schedule of events, and it also rents out poles for catch-and-release fishing at no charge. Lasker rink and pool, which you'll see along the way, serves as an ice skating rink in the winter and a public swimming pool in the summer, and is popular with neighborhood children year round. If you still have energy, check out one of the lesser-known museums on upper Fifth Avenue upon exiting the Meer. The landmarked buildings alone are worth a closer inspection.

Taken for Granted

There are many features of the city that, while intrinsic to daily life, are nevertheless taken for granted. These features are often not as glaring as the more familiar landmarks that stand out conspicuously against the urban landscape, but rather a means of navigating, understanding, and enhancing that landscape. In this section we will see that New York is greater than the sum of its preserved buildings and monuments. It is also the hidden network of its transportation system, its street signs and pavement art, and finally, its people.

Subways

There is no greater slice of life than the New York City subway. Since 1904 it has not only been the cheapest way to get around the city, but is also the fastest and most dependable, operating 24 hours a day, 365 days a year. All New Yorkers share a sense of urgency, so it figures that people from every walk of life would zip through the underground tunnels, from Wall Street suits to Danish tourists to inner-city schoolchildren. The 8,259 subway cars moving at any given time mean that commuters rarely see anyone they know and so are free to partake in conversations without a hint of self-consciousness. It is not uncommon for a subway rider to lean over or even straddle a complete stranger

while engrossed in conversation with a friend. It is also not uncommon for this conversation to involve intimate details about the person's life at a volume that is impossible to avoid. New Yorkers treat the subway as their own personal cars, and assume they have the same level of privacy. The subway is the most honest face of New York City, cross-culturally, and across class and age.

Contrary to popular belief, the New York subway is also just about the safest public place in the city. People are always traveling on it. If anything, as rush hour proves, there are too few trains. But this means trains are full of people even in the middle of the night, in the middle of the week, resulting in a city that is just as dynamic below ground as it is above.

Underground Art
Subway art ranges from performance art supplied by musicians, a cappella groups, and break dancers to the ornamentation on the walls of subway stations. During rush hour in the main hubs, which include Union

Square, Herald Square, Times Square, and Columbus Circle, you'll be hard-pressed to avoid some type of performer hoping to unload spare change from lingering commuters. Sometimes these performers walk through the train cars jingling a cup and singing. For all panhandlers, the city discourages cash donations in lieu of donations to charities that work with the city's homeless, such as Coalition for the Homeless, New York Cares, or United Way.

In almost every subway station there are works of art on the walls, ceilings, or floors and mosaic lettering spelling out the name of the station stop. Some of the more notable works of art are the 1913 Marine Grill Murals at the Broadway Nassau Street Station, Willie Birch's 1995 *Harlem Timeline* mosaic at the 135th Street Station, the mosaic eagles salvaged from an original 1904 station that adorn Union Square, the bronze seating rails designed by artist James Garvey in the 33rd Street Station, the animal motif that graces the Museum of Natural History stop at the 81st Street Station, and the whimsical *Stream* mosaic crafted by

Elizabeth Murray in 2001 along the moving platform at the Long Island City Court Square Station. Additionally, the Metropolitan Transportation Authority's Arts for Transit office arranges the Lightbox Project, a changing photography exhibit, at the 42nd Street–Sixth Avenue, Bowling Green, Grand Central Terminal, and Atlantic Avenue Stations, and Barnes and Noble Booksellers sponsors the "Poetry in Motion" campaign that features short poems on the interior of many train cars.

Some of the most interesting underground art is located in the passages of Grand Central Terminal. Note in particular the northeast passage, linking the main concourse to Park Avenue and 48th Street, and the upper-level cross-passage, linking Madison and Lexington Avenues across 47th Street. *As Above, So Below* is a series of thirteen mosaic, bronze, and glass reliefs created by artist Ellen Driscoll between the years 1993 and 1999. The pieces are based on myths, legends, and philosophies from around the world, and are intended to guide the viewer through the night sky as seen from five different continents. By depicting ancient scenes in a black-and-white photorealistic style, Driscoll integrates the old and the new, and relates the tedium of public transit to the perpetuity of cosmic events.

Aboveground Art

There was a time when the subway entrances themselves were works of art, but now only three of the original kiosks remain: Battery Park, 72nd and Broadway, and Astor Place. If you get a chance to stop by one of these antique subway stations, you won't be able to help but notice the exquisite design, dating back to a time when even the most trivial details of the city were elaborately planned.

In addition to subway entrances, there is a large amount of pavement art around the city that often gets lost in the crowds. New York–based artist Gregg LeFevre is responsible for much of the art that is embedded in the sidewalk. Combining educational and artistic elements, LeFevre created the bronze literary quotations that grace the south side of the New York Public Library on 41st Street between Park and Fifth Avenues, the bronze panels featuring the work of preeminent New York architects that sit outside of 101 Park Avenue where many of these architects worked, and bronze medallion timelines at Foley Square in Lower Manhattan and in Union Square. He has also worked on a number of commissioned pieces both in New York City and throughout the country.

Manhattan Schist

The most fundamental feature of New York City, literally, is Manhattan schist. The geological bedrock of Manhattan Island beneath the city's subway system is the reason for the city's unique skyline. Composed of quartz, feldspar, hornblende, and white mica, the flecks of which gives it its glittering appearance, the 450-million-year-old bedrock is found at various depths throughout the city, from 18 feet below ground in Times Square to 260 feet below ground in Greenwich Village. Tall buildings cannot be constructed where the bedrock is too far below the surface to access because they would lack the necessary structural support. As a result, there are relatively short buildings in Greenwich Village and

SoHo, but skyscrapers lined up like dominos in Midtown, where schist is found close to the surface.

Manhattan schist can also help orient you while wandering in or around Central Park. Here the rocks are sometimes referred to as "sleeping sheep" rocks, and they are often used as resting spots for worn out park-goers. The glacial striations, or grooves in the rock, will tell you what direction you're heading in. The striations run vertically, north to south, so if you are walking parallel to them you are heading either north or south, and if you are walking perpendicular to them you are heading either east or west.

Lampposts and Street Signs

If you're not a geologist and you're lost in Central Park, it is easy to orient yourself with the help of a lamppost. There are four numbers on almost every lamppost in the city. The first two numbers provide the cross street, while the second two indicate the number of that lamppost within that sector. For example, a lamppost with the number 7903 is located at 79th Street. Above 100th Street the same system applies in keeping with the four-digit formula, so a lamppost numbered 1400 is at 114th Street.

You'll also notice green street signs on practically every Manhattan corner, but these street signs can also be brown. The brown signs connote a historic district, such as the Cast Iron District of SoHo, Stone Street in Lower Manhattan, and Henderson Place on the Upper East Side. These districts contain landmark structures that have been historically preserved, such as cobblestone roads, alleys, or buildings with notable architectural details.

Yellow Cabs

Yellow taxis have long been a symbol of New York. Images of New York's streets rarely exclude the distinctive vehicles, and rumor has it that when John Hertz founded the Yellow Cab Company in 1907, he

chose yellow because a University of Chicago study concluded that it was the most visible color to spot at a distance. Over 75 percent of Manhattanites don't own a car, so taxis are a vital component of the city's infrastructure, and on a rainy day a yellow cab is about as coveted as a World Series win for the Yankees.

If you want to get a taxi driver's attention, you simply have to hail a vacant cab (recognizable by the illuminated number on its roof) by sticking your hand out. Drivers are legally required to pick up the first passenger they see. At certain times of the day, such as 4PM, the shift changes and it can be difficult to find a taxi that is on-duty. Be forewarned that at busy hours it is not uncommon to see New Yorkers fighting over a cab.

Mosaic Man
Formally known as Jim Power, the Mosaic Man is the long-white-haired fellow who sits with his beloved yellow Labrador pasting colorful glass tiles onto streetlamps. A Vietnam Veteran and later construction worker, Power has lived in the East Village since the early 1980s, sleeping at times on the street when he couldn't make ends meet. When he started his streetlamp beautification project, the city halted his

fanciful creations because he didn't have a permit. Since he acquired a permit, the New York City Department of Transportation has approved his work on 80 streetlamps. Most can be found between 4th and 8th Streets, between Broadway and Lafayette. Each pole takes roughly three months to complete and many are a tribute to public workers and the neighborhood's local history. If you stop to chat with him, you won't be the first. Neighbors are constantly stopping by to compliment the Mosaic Man on his work and admire his craftsmanship.

Further Information

71 Irving Espresso and Tea Bar
71 Irving Place (between 18th and 19th Streets)
(212) 995-5252
All major credit cards

7A
109 Avenue A (at 7th Street)
(212) 673-6583
All major credit cards

AJ Kelly
6 Stone Street (between Whitehall and Broad Streets)
(212) 425-1700
All major credit cards

Amato Opera Theater
319 Bowery (between 1st and 2nd Streets)
(212) 228-8200
www.amato.org
Consult website for show times.
Tickets are $30 for adults, $25 for seniors, students with
ID, and children.

American Museum of the Moving Image
35 Avenue at 36th Street
(718) 784-0077
www.movingimage.us/
Open Wed and Thurs 11AM–5PM, Fri 11AM–8PM, Sat and
Sun 11AM–6:30PM.
Admission: $10 for adults, $7.50 for seniors and college
students with ID, $5 for children under 18, free for
members, children under 5, and Fri 4–8PM.

American Museum of Natural History
Central Park West and 79th Street
(212) 769-5100
www.amnh.org
Open daily 10AM–5:45PM.
Admission: $14 for adults, $8 for children 2–12, $10.50 for
seniors and students with valid ID, free for members.

Angelika Film Center
18 West Houston Street (at Mercer)
(212) 995-2000
www.angelikafilmcenter.com

The Apollo
253 West 125th Street (between Frederick Douglass Blvd
and Adam Clayton Powell Jr., Blvd)
(212) 531-5300
www.apollotheater.com

Asia Society Museum
725 Park Avenue (at 70th Street)
(212) 288-6400
www.asiasociety.org
Open Tues–Sun 11AM–6PM, extended hours Sept–June:
Fri 11AM–9PM.
Admission: $10 for adults, $7 for seniors, $5 for students
with valid ID, free Fridays 6–9PM.

Balthazar
80 Spring Street (between Broadway and Crosby Streets)
(212) 965-1414
All major credit cards

Battery Gardens
Inside Battery Park on the Harbor
(212) 809-5508
All major credit cards

Bistro Ten 18
1018 Amsterdam Avenue (at 110th Street)
(212) 662-7600
All major credit cards

Boat Basin Café
79th Street and the Hudson River
(212) 496-5542
Open April 13–October 31
All major credit cards

Boca Chica
13 First Avenue (at 1st Street)
(212) 473-0108
All major credit cards

Brasserie 8 1/2
9 West 57th Street (between Fifth and Sixth Avenue)
(212) 829-0812
All major credit cards

Brooks Restaurant
24–28 Jackson Avenue (Pearson Street and Court Square)
Long Island City
(718) 937-1890
All major credit cards

Caffe Pertutti
2888 Broadway (at 112th and 113th Street)
(212) 864-1143
Cash only

Carmine's
200 West 44th Street (between Broadway & Eighth Avenue)
(212) 221-3800
All major credit cards

Carnegie Deli
854 Seventh Avenue (at 55th Street)
(212) 757-2245
All major credit cards

Central Park Zoo
64th Street and Fifth Avenue
(212) 439-6500
www.wcs.org
Oct 30–Apr 1: Open daily 10AM–4:30PM; Apr 1–Oct 30:
Mon–Fri 10AM–5PM; Sat, Sun, and holidays 10AM–5:30PM.
Admission: $8 for adults, $3 for children 3–12, seniors $4.

Cipriani 42nd Street
110 East 42nd Street (between Park and Lexington Avenues)
(212) 499-0599

www.cipriani.com
All major credit cards

The Cloisters
Fort Tryon Park
(212) 923-3700
www.metmuseum.org
Nov–Feb: Tues–Sun 9:30AM–4:45PM; March–Oct: Tues–
Sun 9:30AM–5:15PM.
Admission: $15 recommended for adults, $10
recommended for seniors and students, and free for
members, children under 12 accompanied by an adult, or
with admission to the Metropolitan Museum of Art.

The Coffee Shop
29 Union Square West (at 16th Street)
(212) 243-7969
All major credit cards

Comfort Diner
214 East 45th Street (between Second and Third Avenues)
(212) 867-4555
All major credit cards

Cooper Hewitt National Design Museum
2 East 91st Street (off of Fifth Avenue)
(212) 849-8400
www.ndm.si.edu
Open Tues–Thurs 10AM–5PM, Fri 10AM–9PM, Sat 10AM–
6PM, Sun 12–6PM.
Admission: $8 for adults, $5 for seniors and students with
valid ID, free for members and children under 12.

The Ear Inn
326 Spring Street (between Greenwich and Washington)
(212) 226-9060
All major credit cards

E.A.T.
1064 Madison Avenue (between 80th and 81st Streets)
(212) 772-0022
www.elizabar.com
All major credit cards

Eldridge Street Synagogue

12 Eldridge Street (between Canal and Division Streets)
(212) 219-0888
www.eldridgestreet.org
Tours Sun, Tues, Wed, and Thurs 11AM–4PM, docents on call.
Admission: $5 for adults, $3 for students and seniors.

Ellis Island Ferry

Battery Park
(212) 269-5755
www.ellisisland.org
www.circleline.com
Ferries operate daily from 9:30AM–5:15PM.
Ferry tickets (include price of admission to Ellis Island):
$11.50 for adults, $9.50 for seniors 62+, $4.50 for children
4–12, free for children under 4.

Elora's

272 Prospect Park West (at 17th Street)
(718) 788-6190
All major credit cards

Fairway Café (on the second floor of Fairway Market)

2127 Broadway (between 74th and 75th Streets)
(212) 595-1888
All major credit cards

Federal Reserve Bank of New York

33 Liberty Street (between Nassau and William Street)
(212) 720-6130
www.ny.frb.org
Interactive Exhibit Center open Mon–Fri 9AM–4PM.
Tours are Mon–Fri at 9:30AM, 10:30AM, 11:30AM, 1:30PM,
and 2:30PM. No tours on weekends or holidays. Tours last
one hour and reservations must be made one week in advance.
Admission is free.

Fisher Landau Center for Art

38-27 30th Street (between 38th and 39th Avenues)
Long Island City
(718) 937-0727
www.flcart.org
Open Thurs–Mon 12–5PM.
Admission is free.

Five Points
31 Great Jones Street (between Lafayette and Bowery)
(212) 253-5700
All major credit cards

Florent
69 Gansevoort Street (between Greenwich and Washington)
(212) 989-5779
Cash only

Frank
88 Second Avenue (between 5th and 6th Streets)
(212) 420-0202
Cash only

Fraunces Tavern
54 Pearl Street (at Broad Street)
(212) 968-1776
All major credit cards

The French Roast
78 West 11th Street (at Sixth Avenue)
(212) 533-2233
All major credit cards

The Frick Collection
1 East 70th Street (Fifth Avenue)
(212) 288-0700
www.frick.org
Open Tues–Sat 10AM–6PM, Sun 1–6PM. Hours vary on
major holidays.
Admission: $12 for adults, $8 for seniors, $5 for students,
free for members. Children under 10 are not admitted.

Friend of a Farmer
77 Irving Place (between 18th and 19th Streets)
(212) 477-2188
All major credit cards

Gramercy Tavern
42 East 20th Street (between Broadway and Park Avenue
South)

(212) 477-0777
All major credit cards

Grey Dog Café
33 Carmine Street (between Bedford and Bleeker Streets)
(212) 462-0041
All major credit cards

Gray's Papaya
402 Sixth Avenue (at 8th Street)
(212) 260-3532
Cash only

The Guggenheim
1071 Fifth Avenue (at 89th Street)
(212) 423-3500
www.guggenheim.org
Open Sat–Wed 10AM–5:45PM, Fri 10AM–7:45PM.
Admission: $18 for adults, $15 for students and seniors
with valid ID, free for members and children under 12.

H&H Bagels
2239 Broadway (at 80th Street)
(212) 595-8000
Cash only

Haru
280 Park Avenue (at 48th Street)
(212) 490-9680
All major credit cards

Isabella's
359 Columbus Avenue (at 77th Street)
(212) 724-2100
All major credit cards

Jackson Hole
1270 Madison Avenue (at 91st Street)
(212) 427-2820
All major credit cards

Jane

100 West Houston (between Thompson and LaGuardia Place)
(212) 254-7000
All major credit cards

Jerry's

101 Prince Street (between Mercer and Greene)
(212) 966-9464
All major credit cards

Joe's Pizza

7 Carmine Street (at Bleeker Street)
(212) 255-3946
All major credit cards

Katz's Delicatessen

205 East Houston Street (at Ludlow)
(212) 254-2246
All major credit cards

La Goulue

746 Madison Avenue (between 64th and 65th Streets)
(212) 988-8169
All major credit cards

Landmark's Sunshine Cinema

143 East Houston (between Forsythe and Eldridge)
(212) 330-8182
www.landmarktheatres.com
Tickets are $10.75 for adults, $7 for children and seniors.

Les Halles Downtown

15 John Street (between Nassau and Broadway)
(212) 285-8585
All major credit cards

Lincoln Center

Columbus Avenue between 62nd and 65th Streets
Avery Fisher Hall and Alice Tully Hall (212) 875-5000
The Juilliard School (212) 799-5000
Metropolitan Opera House (212) 362-6000
Mitzi E. Newhouse Theater (212) 362-7600

New York State Theater (212) 870-5500
Vivian Beaumont Theater (212) 362-7600
Walter Reade Theater (212) 875-5600
www.lincolncenter.org

Lupe's East LA Kitchen
110 6th Avenue (at Watts Street)
(212) 966-1326
Cash only

Mama Mexico
214 East 49th Street (between Second and Third Avenues)
(212) 935-1316
All major credit cards

Markt
401 West 14th Street (at Ninth Avenue)
(212) 727-3314
All major credit cards

Merchant's House Museum
29 East Fourth Street (between Lafayette and Bowery)
(212) 777-1089
www.merchantshouse.com
Open Thurs–Mon 12–5PM.
Admission: $8 for adults, $5 for students and seniors, free for
members and for children under 12 accompanied by an adult.

Mount Vernon Hotel Museum and Garden
421 East 61st Street (between First and York Avenues)
(212) 838-6878
www.mvhm.org
Open year round Tues–Sun 11AM–4PM, Tues 6–9PM in
June and July. Closed in August and on major holidays.
Admission: $8 for adults, $7 for students and seniors, free
for members and children under 12.

Museum of the Chinese in the Americas
70 Mulberry Street, 2nd Floor (on Bayard Street)
(212) 619-4785
www.moca-nyc.org
Open Tues–Thurs 12–6PM, Fri 12–7PM, Sat and Sun 12–

6PM, closed Mon.
Admission: $3 for adults, $1 for students with ID and seniors, free for members and children under 12; free on Fridays.

Museum of Jewish Heritage: A Living Memorial to the Holocaust
36 Battery Place (near 1st Place)
(646) 437-4200
www.mjhnyc.org
Open Sun, Mon, Tues, and Thurs 10AM–5:45PM, Wed 10AM–8PM, Fri 10AM–5PM.
$10 for adults, $7 for seniors, $5 for students, free for children under 12.

Museum of Modern Art (MoMA)
11 West 53rd Street (between Fifth and Sixth Avenues)
(212) 708-9400
www.moma.org
Open Sat, Sun, Mon, Wed, and Thurs 10:30AM–5:30PM, Fri 10:30AM–8PM.
Admission: $20 for adults, $16 for seniors, $12 for students with valid ID, free for children and members.

Napoli Pizza & Pasta
33–02 35th Avenue (at 33rd Street)
(718) 472-1146
Astoria
All major credit cards

National Museum of the American Indian
One Bowling Green (near Battery Park)
(212) 514-3700
www.nmai.si.edu
Open daily 10AM–5PM, Thurs 10AM–8PM.
Admission is free.

New York Earth Room
141 Wooster Street (between Houston and Prince)
(212) 989-5566
Open Wed–Sun 12–3PM and 3:30–6PM.
Admission is free.

New York Historical Society
170 Central Park West (at 77th Street)
(212) 873-3400
www.nyhistory.org
Open Tues–Sun 10–6PM; open until 8PM on Fri.
Admission: $10 for adults, $5 for seniors, students, and
teachers, and free for members and children under 12
accompanied by an adult.

New York Public Library
Fifth Avenue and 42nd Street
(212) 930-0641
www.nypl.org
Open Tues–Wed 11AM–6PM, Thurs and Fri 10AM–6PM,
Sat 11AM–6PM, Sun 1–5PM.

Palm Court at the Plaza
768 Fifth Avenue (at Central Park South)
(212) 546-5350
All major credit cards

Paradou
8 Little West 12th Street (between Washington and Ninth
Avenue)
(212) 463-8345
All major credit cards

Pop Burger
60 Ninth Avenue (between 14th and 15th Streets)
(212) 414-8686
All major credit cards

P.S. 1 MoMA
22-25 Jackson Avenue (at 46th Avenue)
Long Island City
(718) 784-2084
www.ps1.org
Open Thurs–Mon 12–6PM.
Admission: $5 suggested for adults, $2 suggested for
students and seniors, free for members.

River-to-River Festival
www.rivertorivernyc.com

Riverdale Diner

3657 Kingsbridge Avenue (between West 236th & 238th Streets)
Riverdale
(718) 884-6050
All major credit cards

Riverdale Garden Restaurant

4576 Manhattan College Parkway (off of Waldo Avenue)
Riverdale
(718) 884-5232
www.theriverdalegarden.com
All major credit cards

Ruby Foo's

1626 Broadway (at 49th Street)
(212) 489-5600
All major credit cards

S'Agapo

34–21 34th Avenue (at 35th Street)
Long Island City
(718) 626-0303
All major credit cards

Sarabeth's

1295 Madison Avenue (between 92nd and 93rd Street)
(212) 410-7335
All major credit cards

Schiller's Liquor Bar

131 Rivington Street (at Norfolk Street)
(212) 260-4555
www.schillersny.com
All major credit cards

SculptureCenter

44-19 Purves Street (off of Jackson Avenue)
Long Island City
(718) 361-1750
www.sculpture-center.org
Open Thurs–Mon 11AM–6PM.
Donation suggested for admission.

Serendipity 3
225 East 60th Street (between Second and Third Avenues)
(212) 838-3531
All major credit cards

Snug Harbor Cultural Center:
The Art Lab
(718) 447-8667
www.artlab.com
Open Mon–Thurs 10AM–8PM, Fri–Sun 10AM–5PM.

Eleanor Proske Visitors' Center
(718) 448-2500
www.snug-harbor.org
Open Tues–Sun 10AM–5PM
Admission is free.

New York Chinese Scholar's Garden:
(718) 273-8200
www.sibg.org
Summer hours: Tues–Sun 10AM–5PM. Winter hours: Tues
10AM–4PM.
Admission: $5 for ages 13 and over, $4 for members,
seniors, students with ID, and children under 12.

Newhouse Center for Contemporary Art
Open Tues–Sun 10AM–5PM.
Admission: $3 for adults, $2 for seniors and children under
12, free for members.

Noble Maritime Collection
(718) 447-6490
www.noblemaritime.org
Open Thurs–Sun 1–5PM.
Admission: $3 for adults 10 and older, $2 for seniors,
students, and educators. Free for members and children
under 10.

Staten Island Children's Museum
(718) 273-2060
www.statenislandkids.org
School year: Open weekdays 12–5PM, weekends 10AM–
5PM. Summer (until Labor Day): Tues, Wed, Fri, Sat, and

Sun 10AM–5PM; Thurs 10AM–8PM. Closed Mon year round except for most school holidays.
Admission: $5 for ages 1 and over. Free for seniors on Wed.
All other gardens and grounds: open Sun–Sat, dawn to dusk.

South Street Seaport Museum and boat tours
(212) 748-8600
www.southstreetseaport.org
Open Apr–Oct: Tues–Sun 10AM–6PM, Nov–Mar: Fri–Sun 10AM–5PM. Closed major holidays.
Admission: $8 for adults, $6 for students & seniors with ID, $4 for children 5–12, free for children under 5 & members.

Sweet-n-Tart Restaurant
76 Mott Street (between Canal and Bayard)
(212) 334-8088
All major credit cards with $25 minimum

Sylvia's
328 Lenox Avenue (between 126th and 127th Streets)
(212) 996-0660
All major credit cards

Temple Emanu-El
1 East 65th Street (on Fifth Avenue)
(212) 744-1400
www.emanuelnyc.org
Tours daily by appointment

Tennessee Mountain
143 Spring Street (at Wooster Street)
(212) 431-3993
All major credit cards

Terrace Café
Brooklyn Botanic Garden
900 Washington Avenue
(718) 623-7200
Closed Mondays, cash only.

Two Little Red Hens
1112 Eighth Avenue (11th Street)
(718) 499-8108

www.twolittleredhens.com
All major credit cards

Umberto's Clam House
178 Mulberry Street (at Broome Street)
(212) 431-7545
American Express and cash only

United Nations
46th Street and First Avenue
(212) 963-TOUR (8687)
www.un.org
Tours Mon–Fri 9:30AM–4:45PM, Sat and Sun 10AM–4:30PM (no Sat and Sun tours in Jan or Feb). Closed major holidays.
Admission: $12 for adults, $8.50 for seniors, $8 for students under 30 with valid ID, $6.50 for children 5–14.

University Settlement
184 Eldridge Street (at Rivington)
(212) 674-9120
www.universitysettlement.org
Open Mon–Fri 9AM–5PM.

Van Cortlandt House
Van Cortlandt Park (at 244th Street)
The Bronx
(718) 543-3344
www.vancortlandthouse.org
Open Tues–Fri 10AM–3PM, Sat and Sun 11AM–4PM.
Admission: $5 for adults, $3 for seniors and students, free for children under 12 and on Wednesdays.

Wave Hill
West 249th Street and Independence Avenue
The Bronx
(718) 549-3200
www.wavehill.org
Apr 15–Oct 14: open Tues–Sun 9AM–5:30PM; Oct 15–Apr 14: Tues–Sun 9AM–4:30PM; extended hours June and July: Wed 9AM–9PM
Admission: $4 for adults, $2 for students and seniors, free for members, children under 6, all day Tuesdays, on

Saturday mornings until 12PM, and during the months of Dec, Jan, and Feb.

Whitney Museum of American Art
945 Madison Avenue (between 74th and 75th Streets)
1-800-WHITNEY, (212) 570-3676
www.whitney.org
Open Wed–Sun 11AM–6PM, Fri 1–9PM.
Admission: $15 for adults, $10 for seniors and students with valid ID, free for members, New York City public high-school students with valid ID, children under 12, and Fridays 6–9PM.

Windsor Café
220 Prospect Park West (between 16th Street & Windsor Place)
(718) 788-9700
All major credit cards

Wooster Projects
418 West 15th Street (between Ninth and Tenth Avenues)
(212) 871-6700
www.woosterprojects.com

Yaffa Café
97 St. Mark's Place (between First Avenue and Avenue A)
(212) 674-9302
All major credit cards

Yama
122 East 17th Street (at Irving Place)
(212) 475-0969
All major credit cards

Zen Palate
2170 Broadway (at 76th Street)
(212) 501-7768
All major credit cards

Zigolinis Famiglia
66 Pearl Street (at Broad Street)
(212) 425-7171
All major credit cards

Bibliography

A good deal of the information included in this book comes from the leaflets, brochures, and websites of individual institutions, as well as conversations and correspondence with the individuals working in these institutions. Periodicals I found most useful were the *New York Times*, *New York Magazine*, and especially the *L Magazine*, which is filled with intriguing New York trivia. I also picked up some interesting facts from PBS's American Experience "New York: A Documentary Film" series directed by Ric Burns, and WNYE's "Secrets of New York." I made use of the following books and websites:

Brockmann, J. and Harris, B. *One Thousand New York Buildings.* New York: Black Dog & Leventhal Publishers, Inc., 2002.

Gray, C. *New York Streetscapes: Tales of Manhattan's Significant Buildings and Landmarks.* New York: Harry N. Abrams, 2003.

Jackson, K.T., *The Encyclopedia of New York City.* New Haven: Yale University Press, 1995.

Williams, E. and Radlauer, S., *The Historic Shops & Restaurants of New York.* New York: The Little Bookroom, 2002.

www.centralparknyc.org
www.forgotten-ny.com
www.lowermanhattan.info
www.manhattanusersguide.com
www.meatpacking-district.com
www.nyc-architecture.com
www.nycvisit.com
www.pbs.org
www.wikipedia.org

Index